T5-AFY-995

CHILD CUSTODY,
VISITATION,
AND SUPPORT
IN TEXAS

CHILD CUSTODY, VISITATION, AND SUPPORT IN TEXAS

———

Traci Truly
Attorney at Law

SPHINX® PUBLISHING
AN IMPRINT OF SOURCEBOOKS, INC.®
NAPERVILLE, ILLINOIS

Copyright © 2001 by Traci Truly

All rights reserved. No part of this book may be reproduced in any form or by any electronic or mechanical means including information storage and retrieval systems—except in the case of brief quotations embodied in critical articles or reviews—without permission in writing from its publisher, Sourcebooks, Inc.® Purchasers of the book are granted a license to use the forms contained herein for their own personal use. No claim of copyright is made to any official government forms reproduced herein.

First Edition, 2001

Published by: **Sphinx® Publishing, An Imprint of Sourcebooks, Inc.®**

<u>Naperville Office</u>
P.O. Box 4410
Naperville, Illinois 60567-4410
630-961-3900
Fax: 630-961-2168
http://www.sphinxlegal.com
http://www.sourcebooks.com

This publication is designed to provide accurate and authoritative information in regard to the subject matter covered. It is sold with the understanding that the publisher is not engaged in rendering legal, accounting, or other professional service. If legal advice or other expert assistance is required, the services of a competent professional person should be sought.

From a Declaration of Principles Jointly Adopted by a Committee of the
American Bar Association and a Committee of Publishers and Associations

This product is not a substitute for legal advice.

Disclaimer required by Texas statutes.

Library of Congress Cataloging-in-Publication Data
Truly, Traci.
    Child custody, visitation, and support in Texas / Traci Truly.
        p. cm. -- (Legal survival guides)
    Includes index.
    ISBN 1-57248-171-4
    1. Custody of children--Texas--Popular works. 2. Visitation rights (Domestic relations)--Texas--Popular works. 3. Child support--Law and legislation--Texas--Popular works. I. Title. II. Series.

KFT1304.6Z9 T78 2001
346.76401'7--dc21
                                                            2001048348

Printed and bound in the United States of America.

VHG Paperback — 10 9 8 7 6 5 4 3 2 1

CONTENTS

USING SELF-HELP LAW BOOKS

Before using a self-help law book, you should realize the advantages and disadvantages of doing your own legal work and understand the challenges and diligence that this requires.

THE GROWING TREND

Rest assured that you won't be the first or only person handling your own legal matter. For example, in some states, more than seventy-five percent of divorces and other cases have at least one party representing him or herself. Because of the high cost of legal services, this is a major trend and many courts are struggling to make it easier for people to represent themselves. However, some courts are not happy with people who do not use attorneys and refuse to help them in any way. For some, the attitude is, "Go to the law library and figure it out for yourself."

We at Sphinx write and publish self-help law books to give people an alternative to the often complicated and confusing legal books found in most law libraries. We have made the explanations of the law as simple and easy to understand as possible. Of course, unlike an attorney advising an individual client, we cannot cover every conceivable possibility.

COST/VALUE ANALYSIS

Whenever you shop for a product or service, you are faced with various levels of quality and price. In deciding what product or service to buy, you make a cost/value analysis on the basis of your willingness to pay and the quality you desire.

When buying a car, you decide whether you want transportation, comfort, status, or sex appeal. Accordingly, you decide among such choices as a Neon, a Lincoln, a Rolls Royce, or a Porsche. Before making a decision, you usually weigh the merits of each option against the cost.

When you get a headache, you can take a pain reliever (such as aspirin) or visit a medical specialist for a neurological examination. Given this choice, most people, of course, take a pain reliever, since it costs only pennies; whereas a medical examination costs hundreds of dollars and takes a lot of time. This is usually a logical choice because it is rare to need anything more than a pain reliever for a headache. But in some cases, a headache may indicate a brain tumor and failing to see a specialist right away can result in complications. Should everyone with a headache go to a specialist? Of course not, but people treating their own illnesses must realize that they are betting on the basis of their cost/value analysis of the situation. They are taking the most logical option.

The same cost/value analysis must be made when deciding to do one's own legal work. Many legal situations are very straight forward, requiring a simple form and no complicated analysis. Anyone with a little intelligence and a book of instructions can handle the matter without outside help.

But there is always the chance that complications are involved that only an attorney would notice. To simplify the law into a book like this, several legal cases often must be condensed into a single sentence or paragraph. Otherwise, the book would be several hundred pages long and too complicated for most people. However, this simplification necessarily leaves out many details and nuances that would apply to special or unusual situations. Also, there are many ways to interpret most legal questions. Your case may come before a judge who disagrees with the analysis of our authors.

Therefore, in deciding to use a self-help law book and to do your own legal work, you must realize that you are making a cost/value analysis. You have decided that the money you will save in doing it yourself outweighs the chance that your case will not turn out to your satisfaction. Most people handling their own simple legal matters never have a problem, but occasionally people find that it ended up costing them more to have an attorney straighten out the situation than it would have if they had hired an attorney in the beginning. Keep this in mind if you decide to handle your own case, and be sure to consult an attorney if you feel you might need further guidance.

LOCAL RULES   The next thing to remember is that a book which covers the law for the entire nation, or even for an entire state, cannot possibly include every procedural difference of every county court. Whenever possible, we provide the exact form needed; however, in some areas, each county, or even each judge, may require unique forms and procedures. In our *state* books, our forms usually cover the majority of counties in the state, or provide examples of the type of form that will be required. In our *national* books, our forms are sometimes even more general in nature but are designed to give a good idea of the type of form that will be needed in most locations. Nonetheless, keep in mind that your *state*, county, or judge may have a requirement, or use a form, that is not included in this book.

You should not necessarily expect to be able to get all of the information and resources you need solely from within the pages of this book. This book will serve as your guide, giving you specific information whenever possible and helping you to find out what else you will need to know. This is just like if you decided to build your own backyard deck. You might purchase a book on how to build decks. However, such a book would not include the building codes and permit requirements of every city, town, county, and township in the nation; nor would it include the lumber, nails, saws, hammers, and other materials and tools you would need to actually build the deck. You would use the book as your guide, and then do some work and research involving such matters as whether you need a permit of some kind, what type and grade of wood are available in your area, whether to use hand tools or power tools, and how to use those tools.

Before using the forms in a book like this, you should check with your court clerk to see if there are any local rules of which you should be aware, or local forms you will need to use. Often, such forms will require the same information as the forms in the book but are merely laid out differently, use slightly different language, or use different color paper so the clerks can easily find them. They will sometimes require additional information.

CHANGES IN
THE LAW

Besides being subject to local rules and practices, the law is subject to change at any time. The courts and the legislatures of all fifty states are constantly revising the laws. It is possible that while you are reading this book, some aspect of the law is being changed.

In most cases, the change will be of minimal significance. A form will be redesigned, additional information will be required, or a waiting period will be extended. As a result, you might need to revise a form, file an extra form, or wait out a longer time period; these types of changes will not usually affect the outcome of your case. On the other hand, sometimes a major part of the law is changed, the entire law in a particular area is rewritten, or a case that was the basis of a central legal point is overruled. In such instances, your entire ability to pursue your case may be impaired.

To help you with local requirements and changes in the law, be sure to read the section in Chapter 1 on "Legal Research."

Again, you should weigh the value of your case against the cost of an attorney and make a decision as to what you believe is in your best interest.

Introduction

There are many different situations in which issues related to child custody, support, and visitation may arise. They may be trying at times. The purpose of this book is to provide you with basic information on these areas of law as well as information about navigating through the legal system. You should also remember that, by necessity, this book is a simplified analysis. However, after reading it, the laws surrounding your children may seem less confusing.

As you read this book, remember that no book that is general in nature can cover every factual situation that may arise. For that reason, you may need to do additional research on your own to be sure that you are correctly interpreting the law as it applies to your particular set of facts. If your situation is unusually complex, you may also need to consider at least a consultation with an attorney to be certain you understand the law that applies to your case.

Keep in mind that different counties may have their own local rules. We cannot cover all of these in a statewide book. Check with each court for the specific rules for the counties you deal with.

Be sure to read the entire book before you begin preparing any of the forms. As a reminder, you will need to modify these forms to allow for the facts in your case and to allow for any changes in the law that occur after the preparation of this book.

Laws can change at any time, either by legislative action or by court decision interpreting the statutes already on the books. Every effort has been made to insure the accuracy of this book at the time of publication.

The book is divided into six sections. The first section contains general information on how to find the laws themselves, do basic legal research, and find and work with an attorney. Section two contains the information about custody cases, and includes information on paternity suits for those who have never been married to their child's other parent.

Dividing parenting time and paying money for the children are essential. The third section contains information about visitation and the standard visitation schedule. Information on child support is found in section four.

The fifth section contains procedural information that applies to all three types of cases (custody, support, and visitation). Section six contains information on enforcement and modification of court orders and on emergencies that may arise in case you need to go back to court.

At the end of the book, you will find an appendix containing sample forms. This section shows how you might fill out some of the forms commonly found in custody, support, and visitation cases. These forms are based on four hypothetical cases described in the appendix and include some of the forms that apply to each case. There is one each of a typical custody, paternity, support modification, and visitation modification case. For your own case, you will need to type your own forms and change the forms to correspond with your case.

Use the sample forms as a guide only; there is no way to draft a sample form that will cover every aspect of every case. This book is not intended to be a complete form book, and there may be instances where you will need forms that are not included in this book. Therefore, you may also want to refer to other, more complete, form books such as the *Family Practice Manual* put out by the State Bar of Texas and found in most law libraries and many public libraries.

SECTION I:

THE LAW AND
THE LAWYER'S ROLE

FINDING THE LAW 1

The law is ever changing. There are many resources in which to find it, and it develops through the courts, statutes, and the U.S. and state Constitutions. This book is designed to give you the basics of the law, but occasionally, you may want to look things up yourself.

LEGAL RESEARCH

Perhaps in addition to a lawyer, you will need to consult your local law library or public library with a legal section. If your public library does not have a legal section, or if it does not contain the information you need, you may be able to find a law library in or near your county courthouse.

If you live near a law school, you will also find a library there.

The librarian will be able to direct you to the proper books, but cannot tell you which forms to use or how to fill them out because they are not allowed to give legal advice. (Some information about laws and cases is available on the Internet as well at **http://www.findlaw.com**, but you will find most of what you need here.)

In the law library, you will find several sets of books that you can use for your legal research.

STATUTES OR CODES

One set of books that you will need to use is the set of statutes and codes. These are the books in which the laws passed by the state legislature are found. In Texas, these books are the Vernon's Revised Statutes Annotated or Vernon's Revised Codes Annotated. They are more commonly referred to as the *black statutes*, because the books are all black.

The laws you will primarily be using will be found in the three volumes entitled the "Family Code". The three volumes may have some terminology that requires a brief explanation here. *Revised* means that the books have been updated with changes in the law. Sometimes, an entirely new book will be printed, and sometimes the changes appear in a pocket part in the original volume or a soft cover book kept near the main volume. *Annotated* just means that the statutes also contain a listing of some court cases that have been decided under a particular section of the statute and a summary of the court decision will also be found immediately following the text of the statute section itself.

Since our legislature meets every two years (in odd numbered years), it is possible that each time they meet they could make some change to the law that governs your case. It is important that you use the most current version of the law. Therefore, when you look in these books, be sure you check for the most current *supplements* to the volumes. Ask a librarian for help.

NOTE: *The librarian cannot give you legal advice, tell you which form to use, or how to fill out a form.*

PRACTICE MANUALS

You will also find practice manuals that contain forms and practical pointers for handling different kinds of cases. There are several different manuals for family law in Texas, including a three volume set published by the state bar called the Family Practice Manual.

COURT RULES

These books contain the procedural rules for court cases. The rules that apply to family law cases are found in the Rules of Civil Procedure and the Civil Rules of Evidence. These volumes are part of the black statute books.

REPORTERS

Another set of books that will be helpful to you is the reporter. These books contain the written opinions of the courts, usually the appellate courts, as to how and why each case was decided the way it was.

Texas cases are found in the Southwestern Reporter series. Federal cases are found in the federal series, but there are very few federal cases that address family law issues.

A case will be cited as follows: *Jones v. Jones*, 750 S.W. 2d 859 (Tex. 1985). You will find the *Jones v. Jones* case by looking in volume 750 of the Southwestern Reporter, 2nd Series, and turning to page 859. (The "(Tex. 1985)" means that the Texas Supreme Court decided the case in 1985.) Cases that are too recent to have made it into the reporter will be cited using the appellate court case number until it is published in the reporter.

DIGEST

One way to locate particular cases that apply to your situation is by looking at the annotations following the statute; another source is the digest. This is a set of books called the Texas Digest and it contains brief summaries of cases and tells you where to find the full text of the opinion. The cases are grouped together according to subject matter. The digest contains an index to help you find the right subject heading.

LEGAL ENCYCLOPEDIAS

A legal encyclopedia can also be a good source of information. American Jurisprudence and Corpus Juris Secundum are two national sets, and there is a set specifically for Texas called Texas Jurisprudence. Once again, the material will be grouped by subject matter. You will find a summary of the laws on a particular subject and a few cases listed.

You may also find other books that have been written about particular areas of the law that may be helpful to you if you need more detailed information on a subject.

INTERNET

You may also access information about statutes and case law on Internet sites such as:

http://www.findlaw.com

Role of the Lawyer 2

As with anything, there are advantages and disadvantages to having an attorney represent you in your lawsuit.

Advantages

The advantages are fairly obvious. An attorney knows the law, the rules of evidence, and the rules of procedure; these are all things you will be responsible for knowing (just as if you were a lawyer) if you represent yourself.

EXPERIENCE   The lawyer also has experience in trying cases, and will know what evidence will be most helpful to you in trial and what evidence will hurt your chances of victory.

Complications that only an attorney would notice can arise in many cases. If you mishandle your case, it may not be possible for attorneys to fix it later. Even if they can, it will usually be much more expensive than if you had just hired them in the first place.

OBJECTIVITY   Another advantage the attorney has is objectivity. You are a party to the case, and, as such, you have a big emotional investment in the outcome. Custody cases also bring out very raw emotions involving the children and the other parties. No matter what emotional strategies are used by the other side, your attorney will be able to help you maintain perspective and help you make decisions regarding your case with a clearer head and with more emotional distance.

CREDIBILITY
AND DENIAL
You may be taken more seriously if you have an attorney. Having an attorney also reduces the chance that you will have fatal drafting errors in your pleadings and final orders. You may be able to keep your case moving faster, since most attorneys have a heavy caseload and sometimes work on your case will come behind work on other cases, but the attorney has more experience in working within the system. And, finally, you will not have to be responsible for all of the administrative details that go along with a lawsuit.

DISADVANTAGES

Of course, this freedom from details comes at a price.

COST
Cost is the main advantage to representing yourself. Most lawyers will charge you an hourly rate, and require some sort of *retainer* to be paid before they will begin work on your case. The hourly rate will vary, depending on your geographical location, the years of experience the lawyer has, the type of case it is, and the complexity of the case.

You should always receive an itemized bill from your lawyer so that you know how your money is being spent. You need to be prepared to pay for all things done by the lawyer that relate to your case. This includes talking on the phone to you and to the other attorney and writing letters, not just drafting pleadings and going to court.

ATTORNEY SELECTION

If you decide that the advantages of having a lawyer to represent you outweigh the disadvantages, you will face the problem of selecting an attorney. It is important that you hire an attorney that is knowledgeable and experienced in family law matters. You also need to feel comfortable working with that lawyer. It does not matter how good a lawyer is if you are not comfortable with him or her. You should feel like all of your questions are being answered and answered correctly. There are some answers no lawyer can give you, particularly as to the final outcome. No attorney can guarantee you what the outcome of a contested case will be, and you should be wary of anyone who says they will give you a 100% guarantee.

If you do not already know a good domestic relations lawyer, there are several sources for referrals.

Friends. One of the best ways to find a lawyer is through someone you know. Ask around to get names from acquaintances of lawyers they have worked with and liked.

Bar association. In larger cities, the local bar association will maintain a referral list.

Employers. You might also check with your employer as many offer a prepaid legal plan or a plan for discounted legal services as an employment benefit.

Legal clinic. If you are a very low income individual, you may also be eligible for services from a legal clinic. Most large cities offer some form of low-cost legal clinic. Of course, you can always check the phone book and the Internet as well.

Internet. Many attorneys have websites with information about the firm and phone numbers to reach them. Also, many websites can help you find a lawyer in your state, such as

http://www.martindale.com

CONSULTATION

Feel free to schedule consultations with more than one lawyer. Many will give you a free initial consultation; others may require a small fee.

You should be able to find out in advance what the charge will be. When you meet with the lawyer, do not be hesitant about asking the attorney about their educational background and experience. You should also come away from your initial consultation with a good idea of how the lawyer plans to handle your case and what you can expect during the course of the litigation. You should have confidence in this person. And, remember, if at any time you become dissatisfied, you can discharge that lawyer and hire another.

FEES

Before committing to an attorney, be sure you understand the fee arrangements. Sometimes, the lawyer may charge you a flat fee for your case. If you are quoted a flat fee, you will need to have a clear understanding of what is covered by the flat fee and what is not. Flat fees will most often be found in uncontested cases, so you will need to know what the fee arrangements will be if the case becomes contested along the way.

In other cases, you will pay the attorney at an hourly rate. These rates vary widely, depending on where the attorney is located and the experience level of the attorney. You may pay as little as $100 per hour for a young attorney in an inexpensive area or as much as $300 or $400 per hour for an experienced attorney in an urban area for a complex case.

Most attorneys will require you to pay an initial deposit, called a retainer, and will bill against that retainer. You should expect to receive an itemized bill from the attorney so that you know how your retainer is used.

You will have to pay for everything the attorney does on your case, not just court appearances. This means that you will be billed for letters the attorney writes, for documents the attorney drafts, and for phone calls.

TERMINATION

If you decide to fire your attorney, you will need to send the attorney a letter stating that you are terminating his services. If you have a written employment contract with the attorney, be sure you have complied with all of the provisions in the contract that related to termination. You should also get a copy of your file from the lawyer.

RELATIONSHIP

Once you have made the decision to hire an attorney, there are several things you can do to make the experience better.

QUESTIONS   One of the keys to a good relationship with your lawyer is to understand what is going on with your case and the law that applies to it. If you do not understand something, keep asking questions until you do. The law can be complicated and you should not be embarrassed if you do not understand something the first time. Your lawyer should be willing to take whatever time is necessary to answer your questions.

On the other hand, once you do understand, do not keep covering the same ground over and over. And do not waste the lawyer's time complaining about the unfairness of the legal system. This is frustrating for the lawyer and costly for you. You are paying for the lawyer's time, and complaining about things that are not within the attorney's control accomplishes nothing.

COMMUNICATION   It is also important that you tell your lawyer everything that might apply to your case. It is much better to let your lawyer decide what is important; things that may not seem important to you may in fact be very critical. If you withhold information because it is damaging or makes you look bad, your lawyer will not be able to prepare properly for your case and minimize the damage this information will cause when it comes out in trial. Remember, anything you tell your lawyer is confidential.

You should expect to receive communications from your lawyer when something happens on your case. Also, you should expect to get copies of all correspondence and court documents on your case as they are prepared or received by the attorney.

THE SYSTEM'S   Another key to being satisfied with the way your case is handled is to
IMPERFECTIONS   be realistic. In many more instances than you may realize going in, the system is not going to work the way you think it should. The law may seem unfair to you and you may not understand why the procedures are

11

the way the are. However, these are things over which your lawyer has no control and being angry with your attorney does not help either one of you. It may, however, damage the working relationship between the two of you. When you find yourself in that situation, do not vent your frustration; instead, accept the situations and do your best to work with your attorney within the system to get the best outcome you can.

PATIENCE

You will also need to be patient. Our legal system will often move at a frustratingly slow pace. In many places, the courts are very busy and it may take a long time before your case can be heard. There is nothing either you or your lawyer can do about this, and you will simply have to accommodate your schedule to that of the court.

You also need to have some patience with your lawyer. You are not the only client your lawyer has, and it is unrealistic to expect your attorney to always be available to you. Lawyers who handle family law cases spend a significant amount of time in court. When in court, they devote their full attention to that client and that case, and they will have to get back to you at another time. When your time comes to go to court, you will expect this same treatment. Your lawyer may take several hours, or maybe even a day or more, to return your call.

THE ASSISTANT

When these things happen, talking to the secretary or assistant can be a big help. There are many questions that this person can answer for you. This enables you to get the information you need more quickly and less expensively.

VOICE MAIL

Many lawyers now use a voice mail system for messages. If this is the case, do not just leave your name and phone number. Tell the lawyer why you are calling and what information you need. That way, if the attorney calls you back and gets your voice mail or answering machine, they may be able to leave you the information you need without a long game of telephone tag.

ORGANIZATION

It is also important that you not become a pest. When you need information from your lawyer or need to pass information to him or her, be organized when you call. Get your questions answered, find out what happens next and when you should expect to hear something and finish your call. Do not make frequent, unnecessary calls, as this just runs up your bill and irritates the lawyer. (The really squeaky wheel does not always get the grease.)

BEING ON TIME   You should also always be on time—both for appointments and for court settings.

Pay your bill on time. Clients who pay on time almost always get prompt attention. While you should review your bill carefully and be sure you understand the fee arrangements, you should not have to discuss each item with the attorney.

ACTIONS   Finally, before taking any action related at all to your case on your own, ask your lawyer first. Decisions and actions while the case is pending are important and can dramatically impact the final outcome.

SECTION II:

CHILD CUSTODY AND PATERNITY

CHILD CUSTODY OVERVIEW 3

Litigating child custody issues can be very difficult. However, learning some of the basics can make this area of the law less intimidating. The following chapters provide information on child custody cases to help you through this process.

KEY FACTORS TO UNDERSTAND

CONSERVATORSHIP

In Texas, we have a term for child custody that is different from that used by the other states. Instead of the more familiar *custody* or *primary custody*, the phrase that means custody in Texas is *conservatorship*. The person with primary custody is named the *sole managing conservator;* the other parent is appointed the *possessory conservator*. If the parties have joint custody of the children, they are named *joint managing conservators.* In that instance, the person with whom the child lives most of the time is said to have *primary possession.*

For clarity in this book, the terms *custody* and *conservatorship* will be used interchangeably, but in court documents and hearings, you will need to use the formal conservatorship designations.

SAPCR

A suit for child custody in Texas is called a *Suit Affecting the Parent Child Relationship*, or SAPCR. If a husband and wife are filing for divorce, this suit is included as a part of the divorce petition and not done as a separate suit. In the appendix, you will find forms for the divorce petition.

BEST INTERESTS   The primary factor in all custody and visitation cases is the *best interest* of the child—who is the best conservator, what family situation does the child work best in, what geographical area is most familiar to the child,etc. Every order must be in the child's best interest; however, the Texas Family Code does not define this phrase. Some factors to be considered can be found by reading cases, and include:

- the desires of the child;

- the emotional and physical needs of the child now and later;

- any emotional or physical danger to the child;

- the parenting abilities of the parties;

- the programs available to assist the parents;

- the plans the parent has for the child;

- the stability of the home;

- any acts or omissions of the parent that would indicate a problem in the parent-child relationship; and

- any excuses for those acts or omissions.

The judge has a great deal of discretion in deciding what is and is not in the child's best interest.

THE SUIT   A suit for child custody is most commonly found in either a divorce setting or *paternity suit*, but it includes any action in which parental rights and responsibilities are being allocated by the court. A paternity suit establishes a legal relationship between a father and his child who is born outside a marriage.

There are some special requirements that apply to paternity suits and actions for custody by nonparents; these issues will be addressed in Chapter 6.

DURATION   A child custody, visitation, or support order lasts until the child becomes an adult (or graduates from high school for support orders), marries, dies, has the legal disabilities removed, or is otherwise *emancipated.* (Legal disabilities refers to the limitations on the rights of minors, such as to sue in their own name without a parent. Removal of disabilities means a court has declared a person to be an adult.)

CO-PARENTING
RULES

Regardless of what the custody arrangements are, there are some general common sense rules for good co-parenting.

- No matter what your feelings are about the other parent, do not make unkind remarks about them in front of the children.

- As much as possible, have the same rules and discipline at each home.

- Communicate with each other and do not use the child as a messenger.

- Do not discuss adult issues like child support and custody matters with the child.

- Do what you can to foster a good relationship between the child and the other parent and do not deny access unless the child is in danger. (If you try to ruin that relationship, you may be successful in the short run but end up harming your own relationship with the child.)

- If you have visitation rights, always exercise them and do not make promises about seeing your child and then fail to follow through. (Your children will be much better off if both parents behave responsibly and make the child's needs a priority.)

NOTE: *Most of the child custody laws are found in the Texas Family Code, beginning with Chapter 101.*

WHO CAN FILE FOR CUSTODY

STANDING

In order to file for custody, you must have what is called *standing.* Having standing means that you fall within the legally defined categories of people that are authorized to seek custody. In Texas, the following individuals or entities have standing:

- a parent of the child (a parent is defined by the Texas Family Code as the mother, the presumed father, a man already legally determined to be the father, or an adoptive mother or father);

- the child if the suit is filed through a representative authorized by the court;

- a person having access to or visitation with the child by virtue of a court order from another *jurisdiction* (a court located somewhere other than Texas);

- an individual who has been legally named as the child's guardian;

- a governmental agency or other authorized agency, including a licensed child placement agency;

- a man claiming to be the biological father of the child (this would be done as part of a paternity suit, also called a *parentage suit*—see Chapter 5);

- a person other than a foster parent who has had actual possession of the child for at least six months, with the possession ending 90 days or less prior to the filing of the custody suit;

- a prospective adoptive parent who has the written consent of the birth parents;

- a foster parent who has had possession of a child placed by the state Department of Protective and Regulatory Services for at least twelve months ending 90 days or less prior to the filing of the custody suit; or

- if the parents are deceased, close relatives like grandparents, aunts, uncles, or cousins.

What does all of this mean to you? Obviously, if you are the child's mother and your parental rights have not been terminated, you automatically have the necessary standing to file suit.

FATHERS
The rules relating to fathers, however, are slightly different; they depend on the legal status of the man. If the child is born during the marriage or within 360 days of the termination of the marriage, the man is presumed to be the child's father.

A man is also the *presumed father* if, after the birth of the child, he and the mother either marry or *attempt to marry* (this is a legal term meaning they go through a ceremonial marriage that is void for some legal reason) and the man either files a written acknowledgment of *paternity*, is named with his written consent on the birth certificate, or is obligated to support the child under a written voluntary promise or by court order. (Texas Family Code (Tex. Fam. Code), Section (Sec.) 151.002.)

A presumed father whose parental rights have never been legally terminated has standing as a parent. If the child was born out of wedlock and the parents never marry or attempt to marry, then he must file a paternity suit, or a court must legally find him to be the father, in order to have standing.

NONPARENTS
Nonparents must comply with one of the other subsections of Section 102.003 of the Texas Family Code. There is special standing for grandparents. (Tex. Fam. Code, Sec. 102.004.) If a nonparent does not meet the standing requirements, they cannot file a suit seeking custody. For more information, see Chapter 6 on nonparents.

STEPPARENTS
There is no provision giving any specific standing to seek custody of a stepchild. Therefore, if you as a stepparent intend to request custody, you must file the suit within 90 days of the date the child last lived with you or you lose the legal ability to do so.

NATIVE AMERICAN CHILDREN
If you are involved with litigation involving a Native American child, you must be sure to be aware of the federal Indian Child Welfare Act (United States Code (U.S.C.), Title 25, (beginning with Sec. 1901).

FILING A CUSTODY SUIT

Once you have decided to file a custody suit, how do you begin? If there has never been any sort of legal custody order covering the child, you begin by filing an original Suit Affecting the Parent Child Relationship (SAPCR).

NOTE: *If you are married, this suit is part of the divorce suit and is begun by filing the custody request as part of the divorce petition.*

If custody orders already exist because you have already been to court on a divorce, custody, or paternity suit, you will need to file a *modification*. If this is your situation, please be sure to read Chapter 19 on modification and follow those instructions for filing suit.

Custody suits are cases too complex to do on your own. While the information in this book will be helpful to you should you decide to represent yourself, you should seriously consider hiring an attorney to represent you, particularly if custody will be contested. Since the consequence of mishandling your case is losing custody of your children, consulting an attorney in these situations is almost always money well spent.

PLEADINGS   Section 102.008 of the Texas Family Code sets out the requirements that must be contained in your custody suit. Petition documents that are filed in court are called pleadings. The first pleading you will file in your custody suit is called either the ORIGINAL PETITION FOR DIVORCE (see form 1, p.136) or the Original Petition in Suit Affecting the Parent Child Relationship.

NOTE: *You will not generally use a Suit Affecting Parent-Child Relationship petition that is not part of a divorce or paternity suit unless you are a non-parent filing for custody.*

The case style. Every pleading begins by setting out the *case style*. You will see this format on every pleading included in the appendix, and it includes:

- the case number, which is assigned by the court;
- the names of the parties; and
- the court and county in which you are filing.

In a SAPCR suit that is not part of a divorce, only the names of the children are included in the style. The names of the adult parties to the custody suit are not included.

Example: The style in a modification of custody suit would be "In the Interest of Roger Davis, a minor child."

You will not know the *case number*, also called the *cause number*, until you file your first pleading with the court. Once it is assigned, you must use that number on every document you file with the court. If you live in a county with more than one court, you will also not know the *court number* until it is assigned by the clerk. This number is different from the case number. The court number identifies the court, where the case number identifies your particular case.

You will notice that divorce cases are always styled "In the Matter of the Marriage of" and never one spouse versus the other. SAPCRs are styled "In the Interest of" followed by the names of the children. In both types of suits, the person who files the suit is called the *petitioner*. The other parties are called *respondents*. In a divorce suit, the style lists the name of the person filing the suit first, and then the name of the respondent.

The proper court. Most counties have two categories of courts—*county courts* and *district courts*. Family law cases, which includes all the types of cases covered in this book, are filed in the district court, and you will need to take your papers to the district clerk for filing. In some moderately sized counties, family cases are sometimes assigned to the county courts for hearings, but you should always go to the district clerks and courts until the court officials instruct you differently.

The appropriate county in which to file your suit is determined by residence. In a divorce case, you must have lived in the county in which you file for at least 90 days. In a SAPCR suit, you file in the county in which the child resides.

In a combined divorce and SAPCR, the divorce rules control. If the parties reside in different states, you will have to comply with the Uniform

Child Custody Jurisdiction and Enforcement Act. (Tex. Fam. Code, Chapter (Ch.) 152.) This generally places jurisdiction in the child's home state, but there are exceptions.

For instance, if there is an emergency and the child is present in a state other than the home state, the state where the child is located can exercise emergency jurisdiction. Another example could be when a state decides to defer to another state to which the child has a significant connection.

Elements. Your SAPCR petition or petition for custody must contain the following elements:

- a statement that no court has continuing jurisdiction or that the court in which the petition is filed is the court of exclusive continuing jurisdiction;

- the name, sex, place and date of birth of the child;

- the residence of the child;

- the full name, age, and place of residence of the petitioner and the nature of the petitioner's relationship to the child;

- the names, ages, and places of residence of the parents, any managing or possessory conservators, or legal guardians not already listed;

- a full description and statement of value of property owned or possessed by the child;

- a statement describing what action you want the court to take; and

- the STATEMENT ON ALTERNATIVE DISPUTE RESOLUTION. (see form 2, p.139.)

Although many of these items are self explanatory, some need some additional clarification.

Continuing jurisdiction. The *court of continuing jurisdiction,* is a term with a legal definition. Generally, a court has continuing jurisdiction if it has either entered a final custody order for a child or if there is a case relating to the child pending in that court.

If that *pending* case is the only one on file and it is dismissed without any final orders relating to the child, the continuing jurisdiction ends with the dismissal of the suit. If there is a court of continuing jurisdiction, all suits must be filed in that court.

Child's property. When listing any property owned by the child, this does not mean that you need to list all of the child's clothes and toys. In fact, in the vast majority of cases, this statement in your pleadings will be that there is no property owned or possessed by the child.

Court action. When you tell the court what action you want taken, this is where you tell the court that you are seeking appointment either as the child's sole managing conservator or joint managing conservator.

NOTE: *You must tell the court what you want. Otherwise the court cannot give you anything. Courts must receive a request before granting an order.*

Alternative dispute resolution. The STATEMENT ON ALTERNATIVE DISPUTE RESOLUTION is required to be filed along with the first pleading filed by a party in most suits. (see form 2, p.139.) There are very few exceptions to this requirement. (Tex. Fam. Code, Section 102.085.) However, there is never any harm in including it.

This statement should be in all capital letters and use the exact words as shown on form 2. This is one of the instances in which specific language in a document is required by the Texas Family Code.

Format. Any pleadings or motions you file with the court must be typed on letter size paper. You should double space everything. You must sign each of these documents when you file them, and, at the end, you need to include a typed signature block with your name, address, phone number, and fax number, if you have one.

Service. Once the other parties have responded to the court, you will also need to include a certificate of service; this certifies that you have complied with the rules that require you to serve everything you file on all of the other parties. Except for the initial petition, which will be personally served, you may serve subsequent papers on the other parties by certified mail, return receipt requested, or by hand delivery.

Copies. When you take your papers to the clerk, you will need to make extra copies. The court keeps the original, and you need a copy for each of the other parties. You also should make a copy for yourself so that you have a file marked "copy" of everything you file for your records.

Fees. For any original pleading that begins a suit, you will be charged a filing fee by the clerk. This fee varies from county to county, and you will need to check with the clerk of the court in each county to get the exact information.

SERVICE OF PROCESS

Waiver. When you file, you will have to include a section on service of process. The Original Petition (SAPCR or divorce) must be served on all the respondents unless they will sign a notarized WAIVER OF SERVICE. (see form 3, p.140.)

NOTE: *The waiver cannot be signed until after the petition has been filed with the clerk. If it is signed before that time, it is invalid and you will have to have another waiver signed.*

If you are a respondent, be advised of the danger of just signing a waiver. If you sign, the other party can put whatever they want to in the order without notifying you. Therefore, you should file an answer with the court. If your case settles, you will then have the right to read the order before it is signed by a judge.

Formal service. If a respondent will not waive service, then they must be formally served. If this is the case, you will need to have the court clerk issue a *citation*. They will prepare this citation and attach it to the petition.

You cannot give these papers to the respondent yourself. In your county, either the sheriff or constable will serve civil citations such as these. You may also use a private process server, but this person must either be already on a list of approved private process servers or you must get authorization from the court.

This is done by filing a *motion* under Rule 103 of the Texas Rules of Civil Procedure and presenting it to the court. Also present an order for the judge to sign that authorizes the person to serve process. The costs for using the county officials and private servers are comparable in most places, with private service usually the higher of the two. Fees range from $50 and up for either.

Publication. If you do not know where the other party is, you can serve them by publication. You will have to prepare and file an *affidavit* showing your attempts to locate them. This is called *due diligence*. (It is best to have an attorney help you with this.) With service by publication, the court is required to appoint an attorney to represent the party served by publication and you will have to pay those attorney's fees.

Additionally, many judges are reluctant to approve citations by publication with the availability of information on the Internet. At a minimum, due diligence now requires an Internet search as well as contacting the person's friends and family. You may want to hire an investigator or use one of the search services for this so that you can show the judge that you made a serious effort to find the missing party.

JOINT CUSTODY VERSUS SOLE CUSTODY

When you file, you will have to know whether you are filing for sole custody or for joint custody. Texas law creates a presumption that the parents should be appointed as *joint managing conservators*, except when one parent has committed domestic violence. (Tex. Fam. Code, Sec. 153.131.) If you want to have sole custody, the burden is on you to prove to the court that the other parent should not be appointed as a joint conservator.

NOTE: *Given the difficulty of getting sole managing conservatorship in a contested case, you should consult an attorney if you are considering asking for anything other than joint conservatorship.*

What difference does it make? As a practical matter, not a lot. The joint custody designation does not automatically mean that the child spends an equal amount of time with each parent. In fact, one parent will be awarded the right to determine the primary residence of the child; this parent is said to have *primary possession* of the child. A visitation schedule will have to be set for the other parent. A contested case for primary possession is handled basically the same way as a contested case for sole conservatorship, and the information in this book applies to both types of cases.

If the parties are unable to agree on a schedule, the court will set one, and it will generally closely resemble the standard possession schedule established in the Texas Family Code.(Tex. Fam. Code, Ch. 153, Sub ch.F.) The rights and duties of the parent who does not have primary possession, but is a joint managing conservator, are very similar to the rights and duties of a possessory conservator. The nonprimary parent will, absent compelling evidence not to do so, be appointed as possessory conservator if the other parent is sole managing conservator.

The primary difference between joint and sole custody lies in the modification of custody from one parent to another. Under previous versions of the modification law, it was more difficult to modify custody for a possessory conservator than it was for a parent who was already a joint managing conservator. However, under the present version of the Texas Family Code, there is virtually no difference between the two.

There are some differences in going from joint to sole and from sole to joint. The bottom line is that, unless there is domestic violence, abuse, or some other compelling reason not to appoint the parents as joint conservators, there is not much point in investing your time and resources in fighting for sole conservatorship instead of joint conservatorship. If you have questions about what type of conservatorship you should ask for, you should discuss the issues with an attorney. For a detailed listing of the rights and duties of sole conservators, joint conservators, and possessory conservators, see the FINAL DECREE OF DIVORCE which sets out these items. (see form 8, p.148.)

Whatever the custody designation ends up being, it must always be in the *best interest* of the child.

PRE-TRIAL CUSTODY PROCEEDINGS 4

Now that you have filed your petition, what is next? This chapter will discuss pre-trial procedures and hearings.

TEMPORARY ORDERS

One of the first decisions you will need to make is whether or not to ask the court for *temporary orders*. These are orders that govern the rights and duties of the parties while the case is pending before the court. You can ask for these orders in your original petition or in a subsequent motion.

If you ask in the original petition and obtain a *hearing setting* (time and date for hearing) at the time you file, you will need to ask the clerk to issue a notice as well as to issue a citation. This is so that the other parties can be served with the notice of the hearing when they are served with a citation and the petition.

There is an extra charge, generally less than $15, for issuing the notice and sometimes for serving it as well. If you ask for the hearing after the other parties have filed answers with the court, you can serve them with the notice by certified mail, return receipt requested.

Either way you approach this, you will need to draft a NOTICE OF HEARING FOR TEMPORARY ORDERS and attach it to either the petition or the motion for temporary orders. (see form 4, p.142.)

NOTE: *When you file the papers, you will need to ask the clerk for a hearing setting. Each county handles this process differently, so ask at the file desk and they will tell you where to go to get your hearing set.*

Temporary orders will include some or all of the following items:

- temporary custody of the children;

- visitation;

- temporary child support;

- temporary injunctions;

- social studies; and

- psychological evaluations of the parties.

In a divorce case, there may also be orders relating to temporary spousal support, temporary use of the property, and allocation of debt payment on a temporary basis. (Tex. Fam. Code, Secs. 6.501 through 6.507.)

INJUNCTIONS There are standard things that are included in an *injunction*, and the language comes directly from the Texas Family Code. Therefore, when drafting an injunction, you should use the exact language of the code unless the judge has ordered something not covered by the standard issues.

If necessary, you can get these orders entered by the court as soon as you file by asking for a TEMPORARY RESTRAINING ORDER (see form 6, p.145.)

NOTE: *You request a TEMPORARY RESTRAINING ORDER in your ORIGINAL PETITION FOR DIVORCE. (see form 1, p.136.)*

This order is effective as soon as it is served on the other party, but it is only good for fourteen days. During that fourteen day period, the court will set a hearing to determine whether or not the order should be made permanent. There is an additional charge for the issuance of a restraining order.

RESTRAINING ORDER The language below applies to proceedings related to the child. In a divorce proceeding, there are other items for protection of the community property that may be used. Property division and protection are beyond the scope of this book.

The contents of the TEMPORARY RESTRAINING ORDER, are mandated by the Texas Family Code and are as follows:

1. Communicating with Petitioner in person, by telephone, or in writing in vulgar, profane, obscene, or indecent language or in a coarse or offensive manner.

2. Threatening Petitioner in person, by telephone, or in writing to take unlawful action against any person.

3. Placing one or more telephone calls, anonymously, at any unreasonable hour, in an offensive and repetitious manner, or without a legitimate purpose of communication.

4. Causing bodily injury to Petitioner or to a child of either party.

5. Threatening Petitioner or a child of either party with imminent bodily injury.

6. Molesting or disturbing the peace of the child or of another party.

7. Removing the child beyond the jurisdiction of the court, acting directly or in concert with others.

8. Disrupting or withdrawing the child from the school or day-care facility where the child is presently enrolled.

9. Hiding or secreting the child from Petitioner or changing the child's current place of abode at _____.

After the hearing in court, these items from the restraining order are now called an injunction.

TEMPORARY CUSTODY

Determining the issue of *temporary custody* is similar to determining permanent custody, except that you will not have anywhere near as much time to present your case. Unless there are special circumstances, many courts will limit the amount of time you have in a temporary hearing, so you need to select the witnesses you will call and the evidence you will introduce carefully so that it has the maximum impact.

Example: If you have several witnesses who can testify about your parenting skills, you should select the one witness who knows the most information. This information must be things that the witness has seen and heard themselves, not things other people have told them. If you have hired an attorney, you will need to give the lawyer information about what each witness knows and the lawyer can decide best which witnesses to call in the limited time you have available. An attorney can also tell you if your case has some factor that would require more time and can help you schedule a longer hearing.

SOCIAL STUDY

A *social study* is a report prepared by a caseworker, generally a licensed social worker, that makes a recommendation on custody and visitation. In larger counties, there may be an established agency that does all the social studies. For instance, in Dallas County, this agency is called Family Court Services. In counties without such an agency, there will be private individuals that prepare these reports. Generally, the court will maintain a list of people who are approved by that court to prepare social studies.

In a social study, the caseworker will meet with all of the parties seeking custody and the children that are the subject of the suit. They will review any records the parties bring to them and any references provided by the parties and any other information they believe relevant. Usually, they will also observe each of the parties interact with the children. Then, they prepare a written report that tells the court which of the parties they believe should have custody. They may also address issues related to access by all the parties to the children.

DEALING WITH THE CASEWORKER

As you might imagine, this report carries a great deal of weight with most judges, and it is important that you make as favorable an impression as possible. In dealing with the caseworker, always remain calm, especially if the child or other parties are present. While it is important to bring to the caseworker's attention any negative information about the other parties that is relevant to a custody determination, it is important that you do not focus only on those issues. This is not the time to vent all your frustrations about the other parties. Be realistic about their strengths and weaknesses as parents; if they have good qualities, be truthful about them.

Also, be realistic about your own strengths and weaknesses. If you know you have problems, take steps to address them before you get to the social study. Remember, no one is the perfect parent. And, in most cases, the other parties are not totally evil, either. It will be better for you if you can avoid being vindictive or angry as you go through the process. If you are having trouble doing this, and this fact is or will become known, you may want to investigate counseling on this issue.

NEEDING A
SOCIAL STUDY

To determine if a social study is mandatory, you will need to check with the court in which your case is pending. Some judges will require you to have a social study in any custody case; in other courts, it will be optional. In a case in which you are representing yourself, you may find it helpful to have a social study even if it is not mandatory.

If the social study comes back as favorable for you, this will help you win your case by providing persuasive evidence that you can use at trial. Obviously, there is a risk that you will hurt your case if you do not fare well in the social study.

The costs for social studies will vary from place to place, depending on whether the study is done by a county agency or by a private individual. The parties usually pay the costs equally.

Psychological Evaluations

Psychological evaluations are a different matter. They are not mandatory in custody cases. Therefore, you must file a motion and give the court some valid reasons to order one. Obviously, if one of the parties is mentally ill or unstable or has been in the past, having a psychological evaluation may be helpful. These evaluations are fairly expensive, so do not request one if it is not really needed.

NOTE: *If drug or alcohol abuse is an issue, you can request testing as a part of a temporary order.*

ATTORNEY AD LITEM

Another issue that may arise at a temporary hearing is the appointment of an *attorney ad litem*. This is an attorney appointed by the court to represent the interests of the children. This attorney will get to make a recommendation to the court as to which of the parties he or she believes should be awarded custody and what the terms of access to the child should be. In cases where abuse or neglect is alleged, or where the termination of a parent's rights is requested, the court may appoint an attorney whether you ask for it or not.

In some cases, the county may bear the cost of the attorney, but in most cases the parties will have to share in this cost. Depending on the nature and complexity of the case, the fees for the attorney ad litem can be significant.

FINANCIAL INFORMATION

For all temporary hearings, you should bring with you evidence of your financial situation. Support is always an issue tied to custody, and you cannot calculate support without this financial information. This includes some form similar to the FINANCIAL INFORMATION STATEMENT FOR HEARING ON TEMPORARY ORDERS in the appendix, and at least two or three recent pay stubs. (see form 10, p.173.)

NOTE: *For information on visitation and child support schedules, which apply to temporary orders as well as final orders, see Chapters 7 and 10 and the standard possession order included in the FINAL DECREE OF DIVORCE. (see form 8, p.148.)*

ASSOCIATE JUDGES

If you are in a county where the temporary orders hearing is conducted by an associate judge instead of the elected district judge, both parties have the right to appeal the associate judge's decision. (Tex. Fam. Code, Ch. 204.)

Your appeal *must* be filed within three days after you receive notice of the associate judge's report and the hearing on the appeal must take place within thirty days. The appeal must be in writing and list the specific findings and recommendations to which you object. The hearing will be a repeat of the hearing before the associate judge, with witnesses called and documents introduced again into evidence. It is as though the hearing before the associate judge never occurred. This is called a *de novo hearing*.

COUNSELING Many judges have now begun requiring parents and their children to attend mandatory counseling programs before a final custody order will be entered. This is not marriage counseling nor is it therapy. These programs are designed to help people be better divorced parents and to address issues that children commonly face when their parents divorce.

RESPONSE TO A CUSTODY LAWSUIT

What if, instead of filing the petition for custody, you are served with a petition? The first step you must take is to file a RESPONDENT'S ORIGINAL ANSWER with the court.(see form 7, p.147.)

DEADLINE There is a very important deadline involved in this process; you have until 10:00 a.m. on the next Monday following the expiration of twenty days from the date of service to get your formal answer on file with the court. If you fail to meet this deadline, the person who filed the custody suit and had you served can go to court and obtain a default judgment against you. This means that you can lose the custody case without having a chance for a hearing.

In order to determine what the deadline is, begin counting the twenty days on the day following the day you were served. When you get to twenty, go to the very next Monday. That is your deadline.

Example: If you were served on June 1, 2001, your ANSWER would be due on June 25, 2001 at 10:00 a.m.

The response you file must be in writing, and you must serve a copy of it on the other parties. Because it is the first pleading you are filing, you must also include the STATEMENT ON ALTERNATIVE DISPUTE RESOLUTION discussed in Chapter 3

DENY ALLEGATIONS
The only thing required by the ANSWER is that you deny the allegations in the petition. If you fail to do this, you can lose the lawsuit. For a sample RESPONDENT'S ORIGINAL ANSWER, see the form in the appendix.

COUNTER PETITION
When you file your answer, you can also file your own suit for custody against the person who sued you for custody. This may be done in the same document as the answer or in a separate document. You use the same form as the petition, except that the petition is now called a Counter Petition. Instead of being the Petitioner, you are the Counter Petitioner. (The other party is the Counter Respondent.) Anything you can ask for in the petition can be included in the counter petition.

SERVICE
Unless you are trying to get a temporary restraining order, you will not need to have the *constable* serve the other party. You can just serve them if they represent themselves or their attorney by certified mail, return receipt requested.

If you also get a restraining order, you will likely want to have the other party served personally. (Even if you do this, you still need to serve their attorney.)

When you are serving a party by serving their attorney, you will need to include a Certificate of Service. This goes at the very end of your pleading, after the part where you have signed. Service will usually be by certified mail, but you may also hand deliver the papers to the other party.

PATERNITY 5

In Texas, the type of case commonly referred to as *paternity* is called a Determination of Parentage, and is governed by the Texas Family Code, Chapter 160. As described before, paternity establishes a legal relationship between a father and his child that is born outside a marriage.

GETTING TO PATERNITY

There are two basic scenarios in which a paternity case occurs. The first is when the child has been born out of wedlock. In that instance, the courts must enter a finding of paternity in order for the father to have any rights in regard to the child. The second scenario is when a child is born during a marriage, but one of the spouses is not the biological parent of the child.

OUT OF WEDLOCK — First, we will address the most common instance in which a paternity suit is necessary—that of the child born out of wedlock. This suit may be brought either by the mother or the biological father of the child. It may be filed before the child's birth, although it cannot be finalized until after the child is born. If you elect to wait until after the birth, you must get the petition on file on or before the second anniversary of the date the child becomes an adult. If you miss this deadline, the suit is barred forever.

OUTSIDE THE
MARRIAGE

Another way your paternity suit can be barred is if the child is born during a marriage but is not the biological child of both parents. If the married spouses divorce and the divorce decree finds that the child is a child of the marriage, once that decree becomes final it is too late for anyone to challenge the paternity of the child. If you are married and have any doubts about paternity, you should deny paternity in the divorce and have testing done.

PARENTAGE ACTION

A parentage action is begun by filing a PETITION TO ESTABLISH PARENTAGE. A sample form is included in the appendix. (see form 17, p.200.) Generally, this petition includes a request that the court establish the parent-child relationship between the child and the father, order DNA testing if necessary, and make orders for the custody and support of the child. The procedures particular to paternity actions are addressed below. The custody, visitation, and support aspects of a paternity suit are the same as those for any other custody suit, and you should refer to those sections of the book for information on those topics.

If you are a biological father filing to establish paternity, you will need to include a statement acknowledging your paternity with your petition. A sample STATEMENT OF PATERNITY form is included in the appendix. (see form 16, p.199.)

A parentage suit may also be filed by the mother or by the Attorney General's office.

CONTESTING

If someone files a parentage action alleging that they are the biological parent of your child, or that you are the biological parent of a child, you have the chance to contest this allegation. To do so, file a general denial but include in it a specific statement that you deny the paternity allegation.

AGREEING

If both of you agree that you are the child's parents, and neither party wishes to have paternity testing performed, the next step is for the two of you to attempt to reach an agreement regarding *custody*, *support*, and *visitation*. At this point, the case becomes just like any other case concerning the dividing of rights and responsibilities to a child. The only difference is that your final order must order the creation of the parent-child relationship between the father and the child. Please see the form for FINAL ORDER IN SUIT TO ESTABLISH PARENTAGE for this language. (see form 18, p.202.)

STATEMENT OF PATERNITY

If the alleged father does not wish to contest paternity or wants to go file a suit himself to establish paternity, he will need to sign a formal STATEMENT OF PATERNITY. (see form 16, p.199.) If there is a presumed father, he must also sign a denial of paternity.

DNA TESTING

If paternity is contested, you will need to file a motion for paternity testing with the court and either set it for a hearing or enter into an agreed order to set up the test. You will need a facility that is equipped to perform DNA testing and that can provide a report in a format acceptable to the court. You will need to find out the names of companies in your area that perform this service. You may want to check with the court clerk to see if they have any information on which facilities your judge prefers to use. You can also check the yellow pages for service providers, ask your family doctor, or check with your local hospital.

A sample Motion and ORDER FOR PARENTAGE TESTING (see form 15, p.198) are included in the appendix. You will need to review Section 160.103 through Section 160.107 of the Texas Family Code if you are going through a paternity test.

The test must be accurate enough to exclude 99% of the male population from the possibility of being the father. If the test excludes the alleged father, all courts will dismiss the case and most will order that the party who made the paternity allegation pay the cost of the test.

COURT ORDER

If you are under a court order to undergo a paternity test, it is important that you comply with the order. If you fail to comply, the court can dismiss the case if you are the party seeking to establish paternity. If you are the party challenging paternity, the court can enter an order establishing paternity.

COST   Generally, the cost for the testing will be split initially and then apportioned at the end of the case based on the outcome. For example, if you requested the test as the alleged father and you are found to be the father, you would be ordered to pay. If you were excluded, the mother would likely be ordered to pay. (The cost widely varies from county to county. If most likely will not exceed $1,000 in any given area.)

TEMPORARY   The Texas Family Code provides for the entry of temporary orders
ORDERS   while a paternity order is pending in Section 160.004.

A father can be ordered to pay temporary child support if:

- he is a presumed father;

- he is the party who filed the suit seeking to establish paternity;

- he has admitted to paternity in his pleadings; or

- he signed an acknowledgment of paternity.

At that time, the court will also order visitation for the man with the child. The court can also enter any other sort of temporary order allowed in any other type of custody suit. These types of orders were discussed in detail in Chapter 4.

FINAL ORDER

In a final paternity order, in addition to the standard orders on custody, visitation, and support, the court will enter an order establishing the parent-child relationship between the father and the child. The court may also order that the father pay retroactive child support back to the date of the child's birth and apportion the expenses for prenatal and postnatal care for the mother and the child. The court may also order that the child's name be changed and the birth certificate be changed to reflect the names of both parents and the new name of the child.

BIOLOGICAL FATHER

If you are the biological father of a child born out of wedlock, be aware that you do not have any legal rights to the child until you take some action to establish yourself as the legal father. This may be done by filing a paternity suit as discussed above.

ACKNOWLEDGMENT OF PATERNITY

There is also another method to establish yourself as the legal father. This is done by preparing a STATEMENT OF PATERNITY as described earlier and filing it with the Bureau of Vital Statistics in Austin. (see form 17, p.199.) They can be reached at:

1100 West 49th Street
Austin, Texas 78756-3191
512-458-7368
email: BVSWEB@TDH.STATE.TX.US

While this does establish you as the legal father, it does not set up custody and visitation rights. For this, you must still file a lawsuit in court. In addition to the forms contained in the appendix, you can also obtain forms for the Acknowledgment of Paternity and Denial of Paternity from the Bureau of Vital Statistics.

PATERNITY REGISTRY

You must register with the state Paternity Registry if:

- you are the father of the child not born during your marriage to the mother;

- neither you nor the mother has filed a paternity action; and

- you want to protect your rights in regard to a future adoption of this child without going to court to establish paternity and access rights.

The Registry is maintained by the Bureau of Vital Statistics. If you fail to register within thirty days of the child's birth, then you lose your rights to assert paternity unless you file a paternity suit prior to the termination of your parental rights.

If you do not register, your parental rights may be terminated without any notice to you. If you do register, you must be served with notice of the adoption suit and given an opportunity to come to court to contest the adoption and seek custody for yourself if you so desire.

Nonparents 6

It is possible for a *nonparent* to be awarded custody of children in Texas. Assuming that you have *standing* to file for custody, as discussed in Chapter 3, you still have a major legal hurdle to overcome before gaining custody. This is called the *parental presumption*. It means that there is a strong legal presumption that it is in the best interest of the child for the parents to have custody. If you are the nonparent seeking custody, you have the burden of overcoming this presumption.

Overcoming the Parental Presumption

You will need to carefully review Texas Family Code Section 153 Subchapter G on nonparents before beginning your custody suit so that you understand what you are facing and what your rights and obligations will be if you win.

CASE LAW   You will also want to be familiar with some of the leading cases in the area so that you can see where your set of facts fits in. The leading case in this area is *Lewelling v. Lewelling*, 796 S.W. 2d 164 (Tex. 1990), which discussed the parental presumption and the strength with which the courts regard it. Start your review with this case and then try to find a reported case with facts as close to yours as possible to determine what the probable outcome will be. You must basically prove that the parents are *unfit* in order to overcome this presumption.

STATUTES

One of the easiest ways to overcome the presumption is by qualifying under the Texas Family Code, Section 153.373. This sections automatically rebuts the presumption if the child's parents have voluntarily surrendered actual care, control, and possession of the child for at least one year. If you qualify under this section, be sure to get your lawsuit on file while the child is either still living with you or no more than 90 days from the date he or she moves out. If you miss this deadline, you lose the ability to take advantage of this section.

PARENTAL AGREEMENT

If the parents are in agreement with the naming of a nonparent as the managing conservator, you can create an agreed order without worrying about the presumption.

SECTION III:

VISITATION

VISITATION OVERVIEW 7

When a court decides custody of children, then the time each parent spends with the child must also be allocated. As part of that process, the parent who does not have primary custody gets a visitation schedule.

STANDARD VISITATION SCHEDULE (STANDARD POSSESSION ORDER)

In an attempt to reduce litigation between parents regarding the visitation schedule, the Texas Legislature has established a standard visitation schedule that should apply in almost all visitation cases. It is called the *Standard Possession Order* and may be found in the Texas Family Code beginning with Section 153.311 and continuing through Section 153.317.

Generally, the parent who does not have primary possession will have visitation on the first, third, and fifth weekends of each month and for thirty days in the summer. Holidays like Thanksgiving and Spring Break alternate between the parents, and Christmas eve and day are split (It reverses the next year where the "eve" parent has the "day").

REFUTING THE STANDARD POSSESSION ORDER

The Texas Family Code creates a presumption that this order should be the one used. It is a *rebuttable* presumption, so if you believe strongly that the other parent should not have this visitation schedule, you can present evidence to the judge as to why the standard order should not be used.

CHILDREN UNDER 3   One exception to the use of the standard schedule is for children under three. If you are in this situation, you can expect the court to make some adjustments to this schedule to allow for the age of the child. Obviously, the closer the child is to being three, the more closely your order will resemble the schedule.

ABUSE   Another instance in which you might convince a judge to deviate from the standard is if the other parent has serious issues with drug or alcohol abuse or if evidence of child abuse has been established. One way courts sometimes deal with these types of issues is to order supervised visits. If the troubled parent has parents who are stable and responsible, and the judge believes that they will do an adequate job of protecting the child, the court may allow those grandparents to supervise the visits. In extreme cases, the court may order the parent to have their visits only in the presence of a therapist or at a facility whose business it is to supervise visits.

The parent seeking to have the visits supervised has the burden of showing the judge why supervision is necessary. Most judges will not order supervised visits unless there is some showing of real risk to the child. The other parent's speculations to what might happen without proof of prior conduct will not be enough. If you want supervised visits, ask for them in your petition.

MOVING   A move by one parent can also affect visitation provisions. There are separate guidelines for parents that live less than 100 miles apart and parents who live more than 100 miles apart. Normally, the parent who has visitation will pick the child up from and take the child back to the primary parent's house. However, if the parent with primary possession moves to a county other than the one in which the visiting parent lives after the order is entered, the primary parent must come to pick the child up at the end of the visit.

If the child travels for visit on public transportation, the court can apportion the travel expenses.

AGREEMENT BETWEEN PARENTS

As with any other type of case, anything you and your spouse can agree to will probably be accepted by the court. If you are representing yourself and the other parent wants to put in the order that you will have visitation upon agreement of the parties or that you will have *reasonable visitation*, you should be aware that this does not offer you any protection at all if the parent with primary possession denies you visitation.

In order for you to be able to legally enforce visitation rights, you must have a specific schedule of times during which you are entitled to have possession of the children set out in your order. You and the other parent can always agree to visitation that is different from that set out in the possession order. However, you need to have either the standard order or something equally specific in your final order so that you have a minimum amount of time with the children that is legally enforceable.

> *Warning:* If you are representing yourself, you need to be very careful if you decide to draft your own visitation provisions and not use the standard language. The rules about enforcing court orders are extremely detailed and technical. A small mistake in the drafting of your order can mean that the court cannot use contempt to enforce the order. If you are representing yourself, please consider hiring an attorney to at least draft your final order.

INJUNCTION AND TRAVEL

As a general rule, you have total freedom when you have possession of the child. However, if there is an *injunction* in the court order, you must comply with the restrictions in the injunction. You may be restricted to keeping the child in a particular county. Or the injunction may say that you cannot remove the child from the *jurisdiction* of the court. This means that you cannot take the child out of state, even for a short trip, without permission from the court.

If you are under restriction, and want to take the child on vacation, you will need to file a motion in court and have a hearing, and get a court order authorizing the trip. Although it is possible for these injunctions to be in a final order, they are usually found only in temporary orders.

The one exception that always exists to the general freedom is any sort of trip that involves leaving the United States. Because of concerns over parental kidnapping, one parent cannot take the children out of the country without the written consent of the other parent. For the exact documentation you will need, check with your airline or travel agent for the requirements.

Nonparent Visitation 8

If you are a nonparent and all you seek is visitation with the child, you must be aware of Section 102.004 of the Texas Family Code. Even though its title indicates that it applies only to grandparents, section b of Section 102.004 has a clause that applies to other types of nonparents. It states that an original suit for possessory conservatorship may not be filed by a grandparent or other person This means that you must either file under the grandparents visitation statute or file for custody (managing conservatorship). You cannot just file for possessory conservatorship.

Since possessory conservatorship is generally the designation used for non-custodial parties, you will need to draft your petition so that you are not in the situation of just asking for possessory conservatorship and visitation. One way to avoid this problem is to ask for *joint managing conservatorship*.

GRANDPARENTS

If you are a grandparent seeking visitation only, you will need to file your suit under Texas Family Code, Section 153, Subchapter H, dealing with rights of grandparents. Grandparents may file a suit for grandparent access to a child without requesting any sort of conservatorship if they qualify under the Texas Family Code, Section 153.433. You will not be entitled to grandparent access if the child is still living with both parents in an intact family.

You can file for access if you can show that the visits would be in the child's best interest and that:

- there has been a divorce;

- the parents have been separated for at least three months;

- one parent is in jail or prison for the three months prior to filing;

- one parent is mentally incompetent or dead;

- the child has been abused or neglected; or

- the child has been formally adjudicated in court to be in need of supervision or a juvenile delinquent.

Before you file, you must be aware of some recent developments in the grandparent visitation area. In June of 2000, the United States Supreme Court issued a ruling on a grandparent visitation case that may affect the constitutionality of the Texas statute. This case is *Troxel v. Granville*, 120 S. Ct. 2054 (2000). If you are a grandparent, you will need to read this case before you file for visitation and check the current status of the law. This case limits the rights of grandparents to visitation. (You can find out more information on grandparents rights from a book devoted to the subject.)

OTHER NONPARENTS

In rare instances, the only other people to get visitation are stepparents. They can try only if the biological non-custodial parent is not seeing the children. Others, such as same-sex partners, aunts, uncles, siblings, etc. hardly ever get visitation. These people either have to file for conservatorship or intervene in a suit filed by the parent with standing seeking conservatorship. This is beyond the scope of this book, and you should get an attorney if you are in this situation. Basically, you cannot get visitation if you lack custody standing (see Chapter 3) and there is no other suit pending (unless you are a grandparent).

SECTION IV:

CHILD SUPPORT

CHILD SUPPORT OVERVIEW 9

In any hearing where child support is an issue, you need to provide information on the finances of the party who will be paying support and on yourself. There is a sample FINANCIAL INFORMATION STATEMENT in the appendix that you can use for your information, but there is no special requirement for the format for providing this information to the court. (see form 10, p.173.)

You must provide the court specific information on your monthly income and expenses. You need to bring proof of your income to court, and you should have your most recent three paychecks and your most recent IRS Form W-2 for this purpose. If you are trying to get child support, provide as much financial information about the other party as possible to the judge. You can get their financial information by using the discovery devices discussed in Chapter 11.

GUIDELINES

The Texas Legislature has attempted to reduce the amount of litigation in the area of child support by establishing guidelines for use in almost all child support cases. (Texas Family Code, Chapter 154.) The code creates a presumption that the guidelines are reasonable and that an order of support conforming to the guidelines is in the best interest of the child.

If the party paying support is a high wage earner, the guidelines apply to the first $6000 of monthly net resources. Beyond that point, the court has flexibility to set the total amount of child support, after considering the income of the parties and the needs of the child.

If you are in this situation, familiarize yourself with Texas Family Code, Section 154.126 before you go to court. You should also seriously consider seeking help from an attorney. While it is possible to deviate from the guidelines in other situations, the party seeking the deviation has the *burden of proof* and must overcome the statutory presumptions for setting child support, which are discussed below.

The guidelines are based on the assumption that the court will order the *obligor*, or the person paying child support, to also provide health insurance for the children.

The guidelines are as follows:

1 child	20% of the obligor's net resources
2 children	25% of the obligor's net resources
3 children	30% of the obligor's net resources
4 children	35% of the obligor's net resources
5 children	40% of the obligor's net resources
6+ children	Not less than the amount for 5 children

If there is more than one child involved in the order, you need to calculate the support changes that will occur as each child is no longer under the order.

Example: If there are two children, the first section will set the support at 25%. Then, put in another section just like the first that sets the support at 20% and have it apply after the first child *emancipates*, or becomes an adult for child support purposes.

NOTE: *No matter how many children are involved, the court will not take more than 50% of the obligor's net resources for child support.*

CALCULATION

In calculating child support, *net resources* includes 100% of all wage and salary income and other compensation for personal services, including:

- commissions;
- overtime pay;
- tips;
- bonuses;
- interest;
- dividends;
- royalty income;
- self-employment income;
- net rental income;
- retirement benefits;
- pensions;
- trust income;
- annuities;
- capital gains;
- social security benefits;
- unemployment benefits;
- disability;
- worker's compensation benefits;
- interest income from notes (regardless of the source);
- gifts;

- prizes;

- spousal maintenance; and

- alimony.

Return of principal or capital, accounts receivable, and aid for families with dependent children benefits do not count.

From the total monthly resources as defined above, the following items are deducted:

- social security taxes;

- federal income tax based on the tax rate for a single person claiming one personal exemption and the standard deduction;

- state income tax;

- union dues; and

- expenses for health coverage for the obligor's child.

Rather than calculate the tax amounts yourself, it will be much easier if you use the tax charts prepared by the Office of the Attorney General and available in Chapter 154 of the Texas Family Code. Be sure you are using the most current version of the code so that you have the updated charts. The Attorney General updates these charts every year, and the new ones come out each spring.

Calculating without accurate information. If the other parent does not participate in the legal process and you do not have accurate financial information on which to base the child support, you will need to base the child support on your best estimate of that parent's earnings. While you should not sell yourself short on the child support, you will need to be realistic about what the other parent is making in the way of income. If you tell the court that the other parent has always worked at a fast food restaurant but you now think they are making $75,000 a year, you will destroy your credibility with the court. If the other parent is not working, set the child support based on minimum wage. Before going to court, review Chapter 15, which deals with default judgments.

MONTHLY OBLIGATION

The child support obligation continues every month. It does not stop just because the child is spending the summer with the obligor. Unless the child is spending almost equal time with each parent, the nonprimary parent will be required to pay child support according to the guidelines.

NOTE: *The person receiving the child support is not required to provide any sort of accounting of how the money is spent to the other parent.*

INTENTIONAL UNDEREMPLOYMENT

If you are planning to avoid your child support obligation by quitting your job or taking a job for no reason other than its low pay, you need to be aware of the concept of intentional unemployment/underemployment. If the court finds that you are intentionally unemployed or underemployed just to avoid child support, the court can and will set your child support amount based on the amount of money you should be making given your work history and qualifications.

REMARRIAGE

If the parent paying child support has remarried, the new spouse's income does not count for purposes of calculating child support. Absent some sort of special circumstance (like an extremely high earning obligor, or a child with special needs, for example) the court will not consider the income of the person receiving support in setting the amount of the child support.

If each of the parents has children from the marriage to each other, there are two options on child support. One is for neither party to pay support to the other. The second is to determine what each parent would owe the other parent and use the net figure.

Example: If the mother had two children of the marriage and her net resources for child support are $1200 per month and the father has one child and $2000 per month in net resources, the mother would owe the father $240 (20% of $1200) and the father would owe the mother $500 (25% of $2000). In that scenario, the father would pay child support to the mother of $260 ($500-$240).

TERMINATION

Unless there is a disabled child involved, the child support obligation terminates on the earliest of the following events:

- the child reaches 18 years of age (however, if the child turns 18 and is still enrolled in an accredited program leading to a high school diploma, the support continues until the child graduates);

- the child dies;

- the child marries;

- the child is emancipated or otherwise legally declared an adult; or

- until further order of the court.

The court cannot force either of the parents to pay for college expenses. Of course, the parties can agree to such a provision and include it in an order.

DISABLED CHILD | If the parties are the parents of a disabled child, the court can provide for support of that child into adulthood.

MOVING | If the parent with primary possession of the child moves to a distant location with the child, some judges will deviate from the child support guidelines and lower the amount of child support to compensate for the additional costs to exercise visitation.

OTHER CHILDREN | If the obligor has the legal duty to support other children that are not part of the litigation, the child support percentage is determined by Texas Family Code Section 154.129, also called the multi-family guideline.

NOTE: *Stepchildren do not count as part of this formula because one does not have a legal duty to support stepchildren.*

Those percentages are as follows:

#of children before the court

		1	2	3	4	5	6	7
	0	20	25	30	35	40	40	40
	1	17.5	22.5	27.38	32.2	37.33	37.71	38
	2	16	20.63	25.2	30.33	35.43	36	36.44
# of other children	3	14.75	19	24	29	34	34.67	35.2
	4	13.6	18.33	23.14	28	32.89	33.6	34.18
	5	13.33	17.86	22.5	27.22	32	32.73	33.33
	6	13.14	17.5	22	26.6	31.27	32	32.62
	7	13	17.22	21.6	26.09	30.67	31.38	32

CHILD SUPPORT ORDERS AND PAYMENTS 10

Every order that provides for child support must also include an employer's order to withhold income so that the child support payments can be taken directly from the obligor's check. All orders must also include a place for payment of the support. It is possible to have the obligor make the payment directly to the other parent, but this is not advisable. It is always better to have the payments go through the court's child support office. This way, in the event of future litigation, there is a court record showing when the payments were made.

If you use direct payments, and you end up back in court because the recipient says they did not receive the chid support payment, you will have to prove that you made the payments and that they were received by the other party. This can be very difficult, especially after several years have passed since the payment was due. All of these problems can be avoided by using the child support office at the courthouse.

CHILD SUPPORT OFFICES

GUARDIAN AD LITEM OFFICE

Some courts will not give you a choice in this matter. They will require you to use a special office, generally called the Office of the Guardian Ad Litem. This is an office that also collects and disburses child support payments. The difference between the Guardian Ad Litem and the child support office is that the child support office serves as a record keeper only. They receive a payment, note it in the records, and send it on. The Guardian Ad Litem also monitors the account for compliance with the court order, and has the authority to take enforcement and collection actions on its own.

Some courts make this option available to you but do not make it mandatory. If it is an option, you should at least consider using it. There is a small monthly fee assessed (as opposed to smaller annual fee for the county child support office), but there is an advantage to having someone monitor the account for you and be responsible for taking the other parent back to court without your having to incur any attorney's fees.

If you need enforcement action and are not happy with the way the Guardian Ad Litem proceeds, you still have the option of hiring an attorney and proceeding on your own.

ATTORNEY GENERAL

If the Office of the Attorney General has been involved in your case, it is likely that the child support payments will have to be made through their office. They will be responsible for collecting and recording the payments and then sending them to the recipient. They also take action on enforcement when payments are not made.

In their capacity as the child support agency in Texas, you will also see them referred to as the IV-D agency and your case may be heard in a court that is designated as IV-D court. This designation refers to a section of a federal law. You do not need to worry about the designation, but just understand that when you see that in Texas, it means that you are dealing with the Attorney General's office.

The Attorney General can be very effective at establishing and collecting child support, but you must always remember that they are a large bureaucracy. This means that, if you go to them to file a paternity suit (discussed in Chapter 5) or to get child support from your spouse without hiring an attorney and filing for divorce on your own, you may need to be prepared to wait a long time for them to get to your case. There is a large demand for their services, and sometimes the wait can be several months or even a year or two.

Once they get to you, they will do most of the work for you, including all of the legal drafting. However, they do not represent either party in a child support case and the work that they will do for you is limited by law and agency policy. They will not help you get a divorce; they only deal with child support and related issues.

DRAFTING AN ORDER

When drafting a child support order, you must be very careful to include all of the required elements so that your order will be enforceable if the payments are not made. The order must be very specific, and must have the method for payment, the amount of the payment, and the time for payment clearly set out. The amount must be a dollar figure and not a percentage. If you make a mistake in any of these areas, later on a judge may not be able to enforce the order by contempt.

CONTEMPT

Contempt is the most powerful tool available to the courts for child support enforcement because it means that they can send the delinquent obligor to jail for failure to pay child support. Because this is such an important and effective tool, you may want to invest the money in having an attorney either draw up your final order for child support or review the one you have prepared. In the long run, this is money well spent.

TAXES

INCOME
WITHHOLDING

Every child support order must also include an EMPLOYER'S ORDER TO WITHHOLD FROM EARNINGS FOR CHILD SUPPORT. (see form 9,p.169.)

This order allows the child support payments to be withheld from the obligor's paycheck. Even if you and the other parent agree not to use wage withholding or the obligor is not employed, you will have to have the order signed. It is then available for later use.

If the obligor is unemployed, the court will still usually order that child support be paid. The amount will be based either on the last salary made or on the minimum wage. The only exceptions are situations where the obligor is totally unable to work and has no income from any source and no assets of any value.

DEDUCTIONS   At the present time, child support payments are neither tax deductible for the paying parent nor taxable as income to the recipient. And the exemption goes to the party with whom the child primarily lives unless there is a written agreement to the contrary.

NOTE: *Child support payments may not be avoided by filing for bankruptcy.*

MEDICAL SUPPORT AND INSURANCE

Another area that falls within child support is medical support. All divorces or SAPCRs should provide for the payment of medical expenses for the children. The standard is for the noncustodial parent to provide health insurance for the children and for the parties to split equally any medical expenses that are not covered by insurance.

HEALTH
INSURANCE   If the custodial parent has better insurance available through their employment, the order can provide that they will carry the children on health insurance and the noncustodial parent can reimburse them for the cost of carrying the children. This reimbursement is considered additional child support as a general rule.

If neither party has health insurance available through their employer and neither can afford to purchase insurance in the open market, you will need to check in to some of the state programs for low cost insurance programs for children. As of the date of the writing of this book, a program was still available. Applications and more information can be found at medical facilities providing health services, especially those that provide services to lower income populations, such as most hospitals, some doctor's offices, or clinics.

UNINSURED Your order should also contain provisions for payment of the uninsured
EXPENSE medical expenses, including time frames for presenting the bills to the other party. If you are the parent who incurred the bill, you should send the bill to the other parent promptly. If you are having any difficulty in getting payment from the other parent, send a copy of the bill by certified mail, return receipt requested. Always be sure to keep copies of what you send to the other parent so that you can prove in court if necessary that you did forward the bill.

If you are the other parent and you know that your child has needed medical care, you should keep up with the bills and be sure that they all get paid. If you do not, you may find yourself in the same situation as many other noncustodial parents who get hit with a large amount of bills years after they were incurred.

If the other party can convince the court that you were presented with these bills in a timely manner and you did not pay, you can be held in contempt of court and sent to jail because these medical expenses are treated as additional child support and not like just another debt that you owe.

UNIFORM INTERSTATE FAMILY SUPPORT ACT

If the parents reside in different states, the Uniform Interstate Family Support Act, found in Chapter 159 of the Texas Family Code, may apply. This law allows states to more easily establish support orders where nonresidents are involved and to enforce orders once they are in place.

SECTION V:

TRIAL AND JUDGMENT

EVIDENCE GATHERING **11**

If you have filed your petition and the other party has answered, you may need to gather evidence to prepare your case. This process is called *discovery*. You will find the rules governing discovery in the Texas Rules of Civil Procedure, generally from rule 190 to rule 215.

If you are represented by an attorney, the attorney will direct this phase of the trial for you. Because the consequences that follow from a mistake in this area can be so severe, and because discovery arises most often in a contested case, you should seriously consider hiring an attorney if your case gets to this point. As you will see from the information that follows, you can lose your entire case before you ever get to court if you do not properly deal with the discovery phase of a case.

An attorney will also be in a better position to know what types of evidence will be helpful to your case and what information the judge is not going to be interested in hearing.

DISCOVERY

Under the present procedural rules, discovery is conducted under one of three levels. These levels are found in Texas Rules of Civil Procedure, Rule 190. The first level does not apply to custody, visitation or support. Unless your case is unusually complex, it will be conducted under level two. If you believe the level for complex cases, level three, is needed, you must file a motion and have a hearing to get authority from the judge to use level three.

The rules have limits on the number of hours of depositions that can be taken and the number of interrogatories that can be sent. Level two allows each party to have 50 hours of oral deposition time and twenty-five interrogatories.

The rules also set limits on the time frame during which discovery may be conducted. Under level two, the discovery period begins when suit is filed and ends thirty days before the date set for trial in family cases.

Since the written forms of discovery generally allow thirty days for response from the other side, you need to be sure you have sent your discovery out in plenty of time for the response to be due prior to this thirty-day deadline.

There are five main forms of discovery:

- the *deposition*;
- the *interrogatory*;
- the *request for admission*;
- the *request for production*; and
- the *request for disclosure*.

DEPOSITIONS   An *oral deposition* is when you summon one of the other parties or a witness to give testimony under oath. Texas Rule of Civil Procedure 199 governs oral deposition.

NOTE: *If you plan on conducting a deposition yourself, you need to study this rule carefully and be sure you understand it. If you miss any of the vital procedural requirements, you may not be able to use this deposition in your trial.*

Depositions must be taken under oath, which means that you must arrange for someone who has the legal authority to administer oaths to be available at the deposition to administer the oath to the witness. You must also arrange for the testimony to be recorded. This may be done by videotape or audiotape. You must be sure that your equipment is reliable and that the recording is audible, otherwise your deposition cannot be used. You must also be sure to comply with the notice requirements in Rule 199 if you intend to rely just on tape.

The other method of taking a deposition is to have a court reporter present to make a stenographic recording of the testimony. If you use a court reporter, you will have a written record of all of the questions and answers, and the court reporter will be able to administer the oath to the witness. Having a written record of all of the witness' answers is a big advantage, but you must be aware of the cost of using a court reporter. Of course, you can use both a court reporter and a videotape or audio recording.

Expert witnesses. If you are deposing an expert witness like a doctor, you will have to pay the witness for their time spent at the deposition. You need to find out in advance how much per hour the witness will charge, as some of these fees can be quite high. You should never schedule a deposition without first attempting to accommodate the schedules of the other attorney or party and the witness. It is much easier to just set the deposition at a convenient time than it is to end up in court over the issue.

Notice. In order to take a deposition, you must *notice* the party you intend to depose. Notice simply means to notify the witness and the other parties of the time and location of the deposition. Be sure to comply with Texas Rules of Civil Procedure, Rule 199.2 on the procedure for noticing a deposition. There is a sample NOTICE OF INTENTION TO TAKE ORAL DEPOSITION form in the appendix. (see form 11, p.176.)

If you are taking a deposition, you must notice all of the other parties because they each have a right to come to the deposition and ask the witness questions.

Nonparties. If you are deposing a person who is not a party in the lawsuit, and you do not have an agreement with them that they will appear voluntarily, you will need to *subpoena* them as well as issuing the notice to the other parties that you are taking the deposition. (See Chapter 14 on the trial for more information on Subpoenas.)

Documents. If you need the witness to bring any documents with them to the deposition, you must request the documents in your Notice and/or Subpoena. This is called a *duces tecum.* You must specifically identify the documents you want the witness to bring; it is not sufficient to just say that you want them to bring all relevant documents.

Objections. During the deposition, there are only three kinds of *objections* you can make. If you have an attorney, the attorney is responsible for making the objections.

NOTE: *If these objections are not made during the deposition, they are waived and cannot be made at any time.*

- *Leading.* The first objection listed in the rule is "Objection, leading." This refers to the legal objection to asking *leading* questions on direct examination. *Direct examination* is when you are questioning a witness that you have called to testify. (When you are questioning a witness that another party has called, that is *cross examination.* On cross examination, you are permitted to ask leading questions.) A *leading question* is a question that "suggests" the answer in the question.

    Example: A leading question would be, "Didn't you beat your child?" That suggests that the witness did beat the child. You can turn this into an acceptable question by asking, "Tell the court whether or not you beat your child." Or ask who, when, where, what, why questions–these are not leading.

    If you are taking a deposition and one of the attorneys objects to a question as leading, you need to rephrase your question into proper form and be sure the witness answers that question. If you do not, you may not be allowed to use that question and answer in your trial.

    If you are at a deposition representing yourself, and it is a deposition being taken by another party, you will want to make this objection to leading questions if that party is suggesting answers to the witness on important evidentiary areas.

● *Form.* "Objection form" generally means the same thing as the leading question objection. This objection is to the form of the question.

● *Nonresponsive.* The other important objection is"objection, nonresponsive." This means that the witness' answer either does not respond directly to the question or goes beyond the information requested in the question. You will want to use this objection if a witness is answering simple questions with a lot of extra information you did not ask for.

If it is your witness, and they have given testimony that is helpful to you and the other party objects on this ground, go back and ask specific questions about that testimony in order to get it into a usable form for the deposition.

NOTE: *You are not entitled to object just because you do not like the areas being explored by the questioner or because you think the questions are not relevant.*

It is important to know what these objections are, because if you do not make them at the time of the deposition, you have *waived* your right to ever make them. You must use the form of the objection set out in the rule for it to be valid, so you might want to write them down, along with an explanation of each, and take them with you to the deposition.

INTERROGATORIES

An *interrogatory* is simply a written question that you submit to another party. If you only want basic information on some areas, this is an inexpensive way to obtain that information.

You must serve the interrogatories on the party, and they have thirty days to send you their answers. In responding to an interrogatory, retype the question and then type your answer immediately after. Sign your answers before a notary public. Texas Rule of Civil Procedure 197 governs interrogatories.

ADMISSIONS

A request for admission is a statement sent in writing to the other party. They must then either admit or deny the truth of the statement.

Example: If you wanted to establish that the other party had been leaving the child alone, you might send the following admission: "Admit or deny that you left the child at home alone from 8:00 p.m. on January 12, 2001, until 4:30 a.m. on January 13, 2001." If you know this to be true, and can prove it, the party must either admit it in the request and allow you to present that admission to the court or create a credibility problem for themselves when you show that the denial was not truthful.

Warning: If a party serves admissions on you, you must be sure that you answer promptly. If you fail to answer on time, every admission sent to you is deemed to be admitted once the deadline passes. This can be enough—depending on what the admissions say—to cost you the whole case. Many attorneys, when they know a party is representing him or herself, will send very damaging admissions hoping that you will allow that deadline to pass.

You can also use admissions to have the other party admit to the *genuineness* (authenticity) of specific documents. This can be a useful tool to simply getting documents into evidence later at trial.

PRODUCTION REQUESTS

A *production request* is a very simple discovery tool, and it is governed by Rule of Civil Procedure 196. If you want to see the documents the other side is going to use against you, you can use this device. You will have to request specific documents or categories of documents as opposed to a request for everything they have. (For example, you can request all documents reflecting income made by the party.)

The only restrictions are that the request cannot be so voluminous that it poses an unreasonable burden. (For example, you could not ask IBM for all of its sales records.) The request must also either be for relevant, admissible evidence or be calculated to lead to the discovery of admissible evidence.

REQUEST FOR
DISCLOSURE
Rule of Civil Procedure 194 governs the *request for disclosure*. The rule contains a list of standard information that any party can request from any other party. In family law cases, the most important of these standard requests are the names and addresses of any people with knowledge of relevant facts (potential witnesses) and the identity of any expert witnesses. In any contested case, you should send a request for disclosure to the other parties. That way, you will get some idea of what the other side will be using to prove their case.

> *Warning:* If a party sends a request for disclosure to you, you must be sure to respond to it fully and timely. If you fail to do so, the judge can keep you from calling any witnesses you failed to list.

As with responding to interrogatories, you must have both the question and the answer in your response.

Unlike other formal documents used in litigation, discovery requests and responses are not filed with the court unless they are going to a nonparty or you need to use them in filing or responding to a motion. However, you must be sure to keep all of these documents in your file for the trial.

BEST INTERESTS

The primary consideration in a custody case is the *best interest* of the child. As you present evidence, you will need to focus all your facts toward this issue. Much of your best interest evidence-gathering will be done using the discovery tools discussed in the previous section. But what kind of evidence are you looking for?

In a typical custody case, you will want to present evidence of the environment the child will have in your home and anything negative about the other party's home environment. You will need evidence on which one of you has been the most involved in the rearing of the child, considering such areas as basic child care, school activities, homework, extra-curricular activities, and parental work schedules. If you are seeking custody of a small child, you will need to address which of the parents spends the most time with the child, bathes the child, and stays home when the child is sick.

CHILD'S BOND

One of the major factors courts use in determining the best interest of the child is the bond between the child and each of the parents and other parties. Of course, the age and maturity of the child come into play here as well. This area is one where the social study can be a valuable asset. The social worker will document the interaction of the child with each of the parties seeking custody, and therefore can provide some evidence of the strength of the relationship the child has with the parties.

CHILD'S AGE AND CHOICE

If the child is old enough, the court can take into consideration the wishes of the child and the opinions they express in this area. Children age 12 and over can sign an affidavit choosing the parent with whom they want to live. While not binding on the court, this affidavit does carry weight with most judges. See the appendix for this form. And for more information on this topic, see Chapter 19 on modifications.

In some instances, the judge may even be willing to talk to the child privately to determine their feelings. If you want the judge to do this, you will need to file a written motion in advance of the hearing or trial in which you want this to occur.

In making this decision, you need to remember that the child will be very nervous in an unfamiliar, adult setting. In most cases, the child is not going to want to choose between the parents. This means that the strong opinions you think your child has about living with you may not be so strong when they are alone with the judge.

FAMILY BONDS

You may also want to address the bonds the child has with other family members.

- Does your side of the family have lots of aunts and uncles, cousins and grandparents?

- Are there other siblings with one parent or the other?

- Is your family widely separated?

● Are there members of your extended family with significant problems, such as drug abuse or criminal records? Will these people be around the child?

DRUG ABUSE   If you have any issues with drug or alcohol abuse or with criminal activity, you must be prepared to address these issues at trial. You will need to show the court, if at all possible, that you no longer have these problems and that your child will not be adversely affected.

ILLNESS   If you have significant mental or physical illness issues, you will need to show the court that your ability to care for the child is not impacted by the illness.

DISCIPLINE AND RELIGION   You will also need evidence on discipline of the child and moral guidance. The courts cannot take religious preferences into account unless there is some element of that particular religion that has the potential to harm the child. For instance, if you subscribe to a religion that does not believe in medical care from doctors, this may become a factor.

FINANCES   The relative financial means available to the parties is not and should not be a factor in determining custody. However, you do need to show the court that you have a stable environment and that you do have the financial ability to meet the basic needs of the child. The courts can address other issues like extras with child support, but the court is not going to want to place the child with a parent who does not have a stable home with some degree of permanence.

If you are in a job that subjects you to a great deal of overtime work or to transfer to another city, you will need to be prepared to have testimony about how this will affect the child.

You will want to gather evidence on the other parent's income so that child support can be set. Tax returns, pay stubs, and bank statements are good sources of information. Additional information on this topic is addressed in Chapter 9, Child Support Overview.

PARENTAL RELATIONS   Another issue that comes into play in making a custody determination is your ability to get along with the other parent. If you work to interfere with the child's relationship with the other parent, this is a factor that can negatively reflect on your suitability as the parent with primary possession. The courts want to do as much as possible to facilitate a good relationship for the child with both parents and minimize the disruption to that relationship. They also want to minimize the amount of conflict to which the child will be subjected. Therefore, if you are seeking custody, it will be in everyone's best interest if you can find a way to work successfully with the other parent.

VIOLENCE AND ABUSE

Obviously, the issues of domestic violence and child abuse may make this impossible. If it will put your child in danger to be with the other parent, the primary concern must be to protect the child. If you or your children are victims of abuse, you should contact the local District Attorney's office and obtain a protective order against the abuser.

If applicable, you need to report child abuse to the authorities. However, do not ever make an allegation of abuse if it is not true. This may give you some sort of perceived short-term advantage in a custody case, but in the end an unsubstantiated abuse allegation can cost you custody and perhaps even access to the child. It also does untold harm to the child to be subjected to an abuse investigation when no abuse has occurred.

For more information on domestic violence and child abuse, please see Chapter 18 on emergencies.

BOYFRIENDS OR GIRLFRIENDS

If you have a live-in girlfriend or boyfriend, this can affect the outcome of your case. In a divorce context, most judges will routinely prohibit you from having overnight guests of the opposite sex to whom you are not related while you have possession of the children. Therefore, if you are seeking custody, you should consider making other living arrangements while your divorce is pending.

Once you are divorced, most judges are not as strict about this requirement, but they will still need to have evidence about your new partner and their fitness to be around children when considering custody and visitation issues.

TO TRIAL OR NOT TO TRIAL 12

At some point in the process, you must decide whether to pursue your case all the way to trial or to settle out of court. For each case, the point at which this occurs is different. Some parties know before the court case even begins that they have an agreement with the other party. In that event, all that will need to be done is to file the petition and draft an agreed order to be signed by all the parties.

Instead of a contested hearing, you will just need to schedule a time to go to court to prove up the orders. (A *prove up* is similar to a *default*, except that you do not have testimony on the terms of the order. You simply testify that there are agreements and they are contained in the order you are presenting and that they are in the child's best interest.) In a divorce, you still have to testify about your residence and the fact that the marriage is insupportable without hope of reconciliation.

UNCONTESTED CASE

Generally, a court will accept an agreement between the parties, but acceptance is not required if the judge finds that the proposed agreement is not in the child's best interest. In reaching a settlement, you will need to balance the time spent with each parent, the need of the child for stability, the child's school and extra-curricular schedules, and the geographical proximity of the parents. If you agree on equal time with each parent, you will want to minimize the disruption to the child.

CONTESTED CASE

In some instances, your feelings at the beginning of a custody case may not be that clear. What should you do in that event?

As a general rule, everyone will be better off if the case can be handled by agreement. There are both financial and emotional consequences to going through a contested custody case. If you hire an attorney, you can easily spend thousands of dollars in attorney's fees. Whether you have an attorney or represent yourself, it will be an extremely stressful experience, not only on you but also on your children. And, in the end, a stranger (the judge) will make all of the decisions about where your children will live. If you can come to an agreement regarding custody you will avoid all of these difficulties.

NEGOTIATIONS WITH YOUR SPOUSE

If you have a decent relationship with the other parent, you may want to just sit down with them and decide who will have custody and what the visitation schedule will be. This is obviously the cheapest and easiest way to conduct a custody case.

It is also possible, if you both hire attorneys, to negotiate a settlement using the attorneys as middlemen in the negotiations. This will save you the expense of a contested trial, but you will incur expenses for attorney's fees. How much depends on where in the progress of the case the negotiations occur and how long the negotiations take.

MEDIATION   If neither of these options is available to you, then mediation is the next alternative. *Mediation* is more formal than settlement negotiations just between the parties, but is much less formal than a trial. In some courts, mediation will be mandatory before the court will let you set your case for final trial. In other courts, you will have to file a motion if all the parties cannot simply agree to go to mediation.

Even if you think mediation will not work in your case, you should seriously consider going even if you do not have to. Mediation can be a very effective tool and cases that no one thought would settle do so a surprising number of times. Even if the case does not completely settle, the mediator may be able to help you settle at least some of the issues. That will reduce the amount of time you will have to spend in trial later and make the job of proving all of your case that much easier.

Mediators. Mediations are conducted by specially trained individuals, usually attorneys. If the court will permit you to do so, you will likely be better off if you can select your own *mediator*. Mediators set their own rates, and can sometimes be very expensive. If you select your own, you will have an opportunity to price shop a bit.

In selecting a mediator, be sure to pick one that has been through the training to do family law mediations. Although the mediator does not have the power to make a decision on the outcome of the case, it is very important that the mediator be knowledgeable about the laws.

It also helps if the mediator has actively practiced family law in your county so that they can give you an accurate idea of how realistic your expectations are. Each judge has different ideas about what orders are best for children and it can be helpful to know something about those preferences when you are deciding on whether or not to accept a settlement offer or go to trial.

If you do not know any certified mediators, most courts maintain a list. Ask the court clerk if they have one. There are also some businesses that mediate cases; some are more expensive than others. Some, like Dispute Mediation Service, Inc., are substantially less expensive than a private mediator. In some counties like Dallas County, you may have a mediation session as part of the social study process. In Dallas, Family Court

Services begins most social studies by having the parties go through a mediation with them.

The rules. There are specific rules that go along with a mediation. The rules are found in Chapter 154 of the Texas Civil Practice and Remedies Code. You cannot use anything you learn in mediation about the other side's case in trial. The mediator cannot be called as a witness in the trial, and you cannot have any sort of process served at mediation.

Format. The mediator is in charge of the session, and will determine what the process will be. However, mediations generally follow a basic format. The mediator will meet with both sides to get preliminary information about the case. Sometimes, both sides and the mediator have a general session together and each side will have a chance to present a brief opening statement. If you are given this opportunity, this is not the time to argue your case or vent your frustrations with the other party. Just stick to a simple recitation of the facts. It is better to be too brief than to go too far in this part of the mediation. If the mediator wants further information from you for the general session, he or she will ask for it.

Next, you will break up into separate groups and the mediator will go back and forth between the two groups. You will need to be prepared in the private session to realistically assess the strengths and weaknesses of your case. Then, one or the other of you will be expected to make a settlement proposal. You may not want to make your bottom line proposal at first since you need to leave yourself some room to negotiate. If there is something that is important for the mediator to know and you do not want the other side to know, just tell the mediator that you want to keep that information confidential. They will honor that request.

The mediator will keep going back and forth between the sides until either a settlement is reached or it becomes clear that there is no way to settle. You are not required to settle in mediation; the only requirement is that you attempt in good faith to resolve your differences. If you do not reach a settlement, then you still have the right to have a trial in court. If you settle, the mediator will write up the terms of the agreement and each of the parties will sign. This will not be a final order, but will be more like a memorandum of agreement. However, once it is signed by all of the parties, it becomes a binding contract and you cannot later change your mind.

After the successful mediation, one of the parties will have the task of drafting the final order and the case will still have to be proved up in court. (See Chapter 16 for information on final orders.)

RULES FOR USE OF EVIDENCE 13

After you decide to go to trial, you should be aware that there are specific rules that govern what kinds of evidence are proper for use in court. These rules are contained in the Texas Rules of Civil Evidence. You should read through these rules and understand as much about them as possible before you have any hearings in court.

> ***Warning***: Failure to understand and abide by these rules may mean that you cannot use some of your evidence.

One of the rules you will certainly encounter is the hearsay rule. *Hearsay* is something that someone else told the witness who is testifying. As a general rule, a witness cannot testify to something that someone else told them.

Example: A friend cannot testify about something that your child's teacher told her. You will need to call the teacher to testify.

Documents can also be excluded under the hearsay rule.

Example: A letter from your child's teacher or counselor cannot be used in court because it is hearsay. If someone tries to use evidence like that against you, stand up and object by saying, "Objection. Hearsay."

Of course, there are many exceptions to the hearsay rule. The most important exception is that anyone can testify to things told to them by a party to the lawsuit. A party is those such as the two parents in a custody trial, anyone who filed a lawsuit, or anyone who is sued.

Business records, like medical records and school records are also hearsay, but they can be admitted into evidence using the business records exception. To get these records in a form that can be used in court, read rule 902 of the Texas rules of civil evidence and follow those instructions.

Another rule you will come across is the *relevance* rule. Every document you use and every question you ask a witness must in some way be relevant to (related to) the issues the judge will be deciding.

Example: If you are litigating a case involving the amount of child support only, evidence relating to the other party's behavior at your child's last soccer game will not be relevant to the amount of child support.

Another important rule relates to *leading* questions. A leading question is one that suggests the answer in the question. Leading questions may be used on cross examination, but not on direct examination. That means that you cannot ask these types of questions when you have called the witness to the stand. You can avoid a leading question by asking who, what, when, where, and why questions or by including the phrase "whether or not" in your question.

THE TRIAL 14

Sooner or later, you will reach the point in this process when it will be time to go to court for your final trial or final prove-up hearing. This chapter tells you what to expect when you get to the courthouse. Obviously, if you have an attorney representing you, the attorney will take care of subpoenaing the witnesses, getting the trial setting, conducting the trial, and making all of the objections. The more complicated your trial, the more witnesses you have, the more important it is for you to have a lawyer. The rules for using expert witnesses and for admissible evidence can be very complicated, even for attorneys.

WITNESSES

When it is time for your trial, you will need to notify your witnesses to be present. The safest way to do this is to get a subpoena and have it served on them. You are not required to have a witness subpoenaed in order for them to testify. However, if they do not show up and you have not had them subpoenaed, the judge will probably not let you get a continuance. If they are an important witness, you could lose your case if you are forced to have the trial without them.

Also, many witnesses will need to be subpoenaed in order to get time off from work to appear for the trial. Expert witnesses will generally require a subpoena. Also, any witnesses you have from any sort of agency will usually not appear without a subpoena.

If you are representing yourself, you will need to have the court clerk issue your subpoena. You will need to get either the sheriff, constable, or other process server to serve the subpoena. Texas Rule of Civil Procedure 176 prohibits parties from issuing and serving subpoenas themselves.

If you want your witness to bring any documents with them to court, you will need to get a subpoena duces tecum and list the specific items you want brought to court. You must also attach $10 in cash as a witness fee to the subpoena.

NOTE: *You should have all of your witnesses subpoenaed at least two months before your trial date.*

TRIAL-SETTING DATE

Some courts will give you a specific date for your trial when you make the request for the trial setting. Other courts will use a docket call system.

DOCKET CALL SYSTEM

A *docket call system* means that the setting they give you will be a setting with a number of other cases set at the same time. At that docket call, the judge will then set the specific date for your trial. Most courts use either a one or two week docket, which means that you will get a trial time sometime within that docket period.

The judge may already have filled the available time slots by the time your case is called. If that happens, you will have to get a new date from the clerk or coordinator. If you have your witnesses subpoenaed to the docket call setting, ask the judge to swear them in. That way, you will not have to have all of the subpoenas reissued and served. You can find out which system your court uses by asking the court clerk.

TRIAL PREPARATION

DOCUMENTS

You should have all of the documents you intend to use organized. And you should know as much as possible about the rules of evidence that govern whether or not you can get the documents into evidence. See Chapter 13 for more information on the rules of evidence.

TESTIMONY

Know what testimony you want from each of your witnesses. Have the questions you want to ask written down before you get to court. When questioning your witnesses, be as brief as possible. Do not ask the same questions over and over to make your point. This will make the judge feel like you are wasting the court's time.

Particularly when you are questioning the other parties, stay calm and stick to just the important points you want to make. This is not the time to ask hostile, irrelevant questions just because you are angry with the other party. Nor is it the time to rehash every old wound and every bad thing they might have done.

Focus on things that negatively affect the children or adversely reflect on the other's ability to care for the children. If they have good qualities, do not be afraid to admit this to the judge. Most judges will give the rest of your testimony more credibility if you are honest about their strengths and weaknesses. If you try to paint the other party as totally evil when they are not, you ultimately weaken the rest of your evidence.

NOTE: *If you want the child to be able to talk to the judge privately, you will need to file a motion in advance. (see form 12, p.178.)*

Before the trial or hearing, be sure you find out everything you can about what the witnesses are going to say in court. Never make assumptions about this. The surest way to lose your case is to have surprise testimony from a witnesses. You should never ask a witness in court a question to which you do not already know the answer. Sometimes, a witness will tell you one thing when you talk to them and testify to something else in court. One way to avoid this is to take the witness' deposition. If you decide this is too expensive, you can ask the witness to sign a witness statement containing the facts they have told you. You might also take a third party with you to witness what is said.

Expert testimony. If you are using an expert witness, be sure to have their qualifications available. You will need to ask them questions at the beginning of their testimony about their education, the professional licenses they hold, and their professional experience. This is called *qualifying the witness*, and it must be done at the beginning to establish the expert's ability to testify to expert opinions in your case.

If the expert witness is a doctor, you will need to make arrangements months in advance if you want the doctor to testify in court. You also need to be sure the doctor is willing to do this, and to determine the fee they will charge. Most doctors do not like to take time away from their medical practices to come to court, and they may charge you an exorbitant fee to appear. At a minimum, they will charge several hundred dollars per hour.

You may have to obtain doctor's testimony by deposition and just use the deposition at the trial. In that situation, you should videotape the deposition so that the judge or jury can see the doctor and not just listen to a reading of the transcript.

BURDEN OF PROOF
The party seeking relief has the burden of proof on that claim for relief. In all cases except termination, the burden is *preponderance of the evidence*. This means that it is more likely than not that a fact is true. This burden of proof is often described as a set of scales with both sides being totally equal. A preponderance of the evidence means that there is one extra grain of sand on one side.

THE JUDGE
If you represent yourself, the judge may be helpful in guiding you through the trial procedures. If so, just follow his or her lead. Most trials follow the same format.

COURTROOM MANNERS

When you go to court, you should always be respectful. Remember, the judge will be making a decision that greatly impacts your relationship with your children. You may only have one hearing in court and only one chance to make a favorable impression on the judge. It is never a good idea to make the judge angry by being disrespectful, either to the judge, to a witness, or to another party.

LANGUAGE

Always remain calm; never shout in court. Do not use any inappropriate language, either. Swearing, cursing, or other crude language will not favorably impress the judge.

FOOD AND CLOTHING

When you go to court, always dress nicely. Shorts, sweat suits, and t-shirts are not appropriate. One should not wear hats or caps in the courtroom. Do not bring food or drinks with you to court.

CHILDREN

Unless they are going to testify, leave your children at home. Most judges will not allow them to be in the courtroom while the case is being heard and they do not need to be unsupervised in the halls.

WAITING

While you are waiting in the courtroom for your case to be heard, you should be quiet any time the judge is on the bench. If you need to talk to the other party or your lawyer, go outside to the hall. Also, while court is in session, do not sit in the courtroom and read things like the newspaper.

ADDRESSING THE JUDGE

Any time the judge comes into or leaves the courtroom, you should stand up. You should also stand up any time you address the judge. Always refer to the judge as "Your Honor," no matter what you hear other attorneys say. Many will address the judge as "Judge." Even though it is frequently done, it is incorrect. Never argue with the judge or another party or their attorney. When stating your position, talk to the judge and not to the other party. And always listen carefully to any instructions given to you by the judge and follow them. Remember that the judge is in complete control of the courtroom and the outcome of your case. While you are in a judge's court, his or her word is law.

ELECTRONIC
DEVICES

Always be sure your cell phones and pagers are off. If they sound audibly in court, many judges will confiscate the device and make you pay a fine to get it back.

TRIAL PROCEDURE

The person who filed the original pleading (the petitioner, usually) will go first in each step.

OPENING
STATEMENT

At the beginning, you may be given an opportunity to make an *opening statement*. If so, you should make a brief statement telling the judge what the issues are and what you want the final decision to be. (This is not the time to argue your case or go over all of the facts.) Not all judges will let you make an opening statement. If you are unsure about this, you have to go first, and the judge does not give you any guidance, just ask the judge whether you should make an opening statement or not.

PETITIONER'S
CASE

Once the opening statements have been made, the petitioner begins presenting his case. With each witness, the party who called the witness asks questions first. This is called the *direct examination*. When you have finished with your questions, tell the judge that you pass the witness. Then, the other party has a chance to ask questions. This is called *cross examination*. Some judges will let you ask additional questions, called *re-direct* and *re-cross*.

RESPONDENT'S
CASE

Once the petitioner has finished with all of his witnesses, then the other party gets to call his witnesses. The same process is followed, with direct and then cross examination. When you have finished with your presentation, tell the judge that you rest your case. Some judges will give the petitioner an opportunity to present *rebuttal witnesses* after the respondent has rested. Once both sides have completely finished their presentations, you will tell the judge that you close.

SELF-REPRESENTATION
AND TESTIMONY

If you are representing yourself, and you are going to testify, make your presentation as well organized and concise as possible. In your testimony, be sure to tell the judge what decision you want made. For example, you might close your testimony by saying that you are asking for joint managing conservatorship with primary possession, and child support from the other parent.

FINAL
ARGUMENT

After both sides have closed, the judge may give you a chance to make a final argument. In this argument, review your most important points for the judge and ask him or her to do whatever you want done.

Not all judges will give you a chance for a final argument. If they do not hear argument, the trial will be over after the last witness has been called. Most of the time, the judge will then announce the decision.

FINAL ORDER

Generally, the winning party will be responsible for drafting the final order. Depending on the type of case, you will need to follow the guidelines for final orders in Chapter 16. Before the judge signs the order, each party or their attorney gets an opportunity to review the order and make any objections. This is not the place to object to the decision that the judge made; the only valid objections are that the draft of the order does not correctly set out the judge's decision or has some other legal deficiency.

Once everyone has agreed to the form of the order and signed it, it is submitted to the judge to be signed. You should always submit the original and several copies (at least 4) of the order. In some cases, the clerk will keep some copies of the order, for example, to send to the child support division. Once the order has been signed by the judge, the case is over. At that point, the only way to overturn the judge's decision is to appeal.

APPEALS

The appeals process, which includes many strict deadlines, is not covered by this book and you will need to research this independently if it becomes an issue in your case.

The main thing to remember in considering an appeal is that you can generally appeal only issues of law and not fact. This means that if the judge finds that the facts of the case do not warrant the outcome you want, and there are no legal errors in the decisions made by the judge, then there is nothing for you to appeal. An appeals court's role is not to substitute its judgment of the facts for that of the trial court.

What can be appealed is if the judge makes an error in interpreting the law, such as:

- ruling that a law is unconstitutional;

- ruling that a law does not apply to certain parties when it actually does;

- allowing evidence to be admitted when the rules of evidence really prohibit its use; or

- refusing to allow valid evidence in.

DEFAULT JUDGMENTS 15

Sometimes, you properly serve the people you have filed suit against, and the deadline for them to file their answer with the court has passed. They have failed to answer, and you may go to court to request a *default judgment*. You will need to call the court clerk or coordinator to find out the court's procedure for defaults. Some courts will give you a specific date and time for the hearing; other courts will hear these types of uncontested matters on a first come-first serve basis at certain times and on certain days.

Once you have determined the procedure, you will need to prepare a JUDGMENT to take with you to the hearing. You can adapt any of the sample final orders in the appendix. (FINAL DECREE OF DIVORCE (form 8) or FINAL ORDER IN SUIT TO ESTABLISH PARENTAGE (form 18) for this purpose. In the "appearances" section of the judgment, you will say that you appeared in person and that the other person, although duly served and cited, failed to appear and wholly defaulted.

TESTIMONY

When you go before the judge, you will need to testify to the facts you have alleged in your petition. Therefore, be sure to take a copy of the petition with you to the hearing. You do not need to read the petition to the judge, but you need to tell the judge what your relationship is to the child (for example, that you are the mother or the father). (If you are not a parent, you need to tell the judge how you qualify for *standing*.) Then, you need to tell the judge that it is in the child's best interest for you to be appointed as the *conservator*. If you are asking for sole managing conservatorship, you will need to testify to the facts that will convince the judge that the other parent should not be named as a joint conservator.

If you are gaining custody as part of a divorce, you will also need to testify to the *jurisdictional facts* (that you have been a resident of the State of Texas for at least six months and of the county in which you filed for at least 90 days). You will also testify to the *grounds* for the divorce (that your marriage has become insupportable because of discord or conflict of personalities that destroy the legitimate ends of the marriage relationship and that there is no reasonable expectation of reconciliation).

CHILD SUPPORT

Your judgment should contain provisions for child support. Since it is a default judgment, you will need to put in a specific amount and you may not have accurate income information. To calculate the child support, use the best estimate you have for the other parent's income and apply the guidelines. At the very least, you should apply the guidelines to the minimum wage amount for a 40 hour week.

When you testify, tell the judge what you know about the other parent's income and job situation. For more information on calculating child support, please refer to Chapter 9.

VISITATION

You must also have visitation provisions. In most courts, unless you are putting in something that is not part of the standard possession order, you will not need any testimony about this part of the order other than to say the order provides for access to the child for the other party. For more information on visitation, see Chapters 7 and 8.

PROCEDURE

Be sure to take several extra copies of the order. The clerk will keep at least one copy, and sometimes more. You will also want a copy for yourself that has the judge's signature or signature stamp on it. This is called a *conformed copy*.

You will also need to take with you a default certificate of last known address. All this does is give the clerk the last known mailing address for any party who has defaulted. Some counties may have a form available for this, but in others you will be required to have one with you.

This certificate is required because the clerks have the duty to send a copy of the default judgment to the party who is in default. There is a sample Certificate of Service in the appendix at the end of many of the forms.

FINAL ORDERS 16

The type of final order you will need depends on what sort of case is filed. A divorce is concluded by a FINAL DECREE OF DIVORCE, a SAPCR by an ORDER IN SUIT AFFECTING PARENT-CHILD RELATIONSHIP, a modification by an order Modifying Prior Order, a contempt by Order Holding Respondent in Contempt.

All orders must be seen by all parties before the judge will sign. It is best if all parties sign off on the order, but if you are unable to obtain signatures, you can send the order to the court with a copy to all other parties. Give the other parties a certain amount of time to object to the order (often 10 days). If no objections are presented, then the judge will sign the order after the time elapses.

Usually, the party who wins is responsible for preparing the final order. You will need to send in at least four copies of the order to the judge, because the court will keep some copies and you will need to get a conformed copy back. If you are the one who submitted the order to the court, you are also responsible for sending *conformed* copies to all of the other parties in the case. (Conformed copies are those that the clerks stamp with judge's signatures or sign.)

If someone presents an order to you based on a contested hearing, your only available objection to the order is that it does not comply with the ruling announced by the judge.

FORMS

There are samples of various types of orders in the appendix and information on specifics of different types of orders throughout the book.

You will notice in the sample forms that there is a large block of text that is in bold type and all capital letters. This is a statutory warning that must be included in final orders, and the Texas Family Code sets out the language that must be contained in the warning and the bold, capital letter format. Notice that the orders contain information about each of the parties. This is also a requirement of the Texas Family Code.

Another item you will see in the sample is a restriction on the residence of the child. Not all courts require this restriction, but some will. Ask the clerk of your court to see if the judge requires any sort of limitation like this.

SECTION VI:

ENFORCING AND CHANGING CUSTODY, VISITATION, AND SUPPORT COURT ORDERS

ENFORCEMENT 17

Any final court order, including those for custody, visitation, and support, can be enforced. The particular type of enforcement remedy available sometimes depends on what kind of order you are trying to enforce, while some remedies apply to all three types of orders. Enforcement actions are governed by Chapter 157 of the Texas Family Code. Chapter 158 contains some provisions that are helpful in child support collections efforts.

The most common type of remedy, which is used to enforce all types of court orders, is *contempt*. The case is begun with a motion for contempt setting out the provisions of the court order that have been violated and the way in which they were violated. Because the rules that apply to contempt actions are very strict, this is an area of law in which you should seriously consider hiring an attorney. For a child support case, you can also request help from the Attorney General's child support collection division. It is very important that the motion be done correctly; if it is not, the judge may not be able to send the party who is violating the court order to jail.

RESPONDING TO A MOTION

If you are served with a motion for contempt, you should hire an attorney to represent you. Contempt is a serious remedy. If the court finds that you have violated a court order and are in contempt of court, you can be sent to jail for up to six months. If you cannot afford an attorney, ask the judge to appoint one for you. It is very important that you do not just ignore this court proceeding. If you are served to appear in court on a motion for contempt and you do not appear in court at the time set out in the notice, the judge will issue a warrant for your arrest.

DEFENSES TO CONTEMPT ACTIONS

There are very few defenses to contempt actions, other than the obvious one that you did not violate the court order. For child support motions, the only defenses are that you were completely unable to pay or that you had actual care, control, and possession of the child during the period that payments were not made. Inability to pay is very difficult to prove, as you must show that you have no money available to pay through no fault of your own, and no place to obtain the money.

> *Warning*: It is not a defense to a child support contempt motion that you are not getting visitation with the child. It is not a defense to a denial of visitation contempt motion that you are not receiving child support. Visitation and child support operate completely independently of each other. You still have to pay child support even if you never see the child and you still have to allow visitation even if you are not receiving child support.

CHILD SUPPORT INTEREST

All past due child support arrearages accrue interest once they are not paid when due. All payments due on or after September 1, 1999 accrue interest at the rate of 12% simple interest per year from the date the payment is delinquent until either the date the child support is paid or the arrearages are confirmed and reduced to money judgment.

For payments due prior to this date, you will need to refer to the version of Section 157.265 of the Texas Family Code that was in effect on the date the child support payments became delinquent. Once reduced to a money judgment, the judgment accrues interest at 12% simple interest per year until paid.

MONEY JUDGMENT

Once you have a money judgment, you can use all of the standard judgment collection remedies to collect.

GARNISHMENT

If you know where the parent who owes the child support maintains their bank accounts, you can ask the district clerk to issue a writ of garnishment to be served against the bank. If there is any money in the account, you will get it, but you will have to pay some attorney's fees out of the money for the bank's attorney.

Before taking this action, you should verify that there is a fairly substantial amount in the account. Otherwise, by the time you pay the fees to the clerk to request the writ, pay to have the writ served on the bank, and then pay the bank's lawyer, there will not be any money left for you and you will be out all of the money you have spent.

WAGE WITHHOLDING

Unlike regular judgments, child support judgments can also be collected by *wage withholding*. At the hearing, ask the court to sign an Employer's Order to Withhold Income at the same time the other orders are signed. This order is just like the order in the standard child support case, except that you will need to add in an amount per month that is to be withheld to pay on the arrearages. The employer can withhold up to 50% of the pay for child support orders.

ABSTRACT OF JUDGMENT

If you get a money judgment, you should also pay to have the clerk issue an abstract of judgment and record it in the deed records of any county in which the respondent lives or owns property. That way, if any real property other than the homestead is sold, you will be paid the child support out of the proceeds of the sale.

TAX REFUNDS

You can also request that any tax refunds due to the respondent be seized to satisfy the past due child support. In order to do this, contact the Office of the Attorney General; they will have the information on how you do this. You will need to start very early in the year for this; likely in the spring to obtain the following year's tax refund.

CHILD SUPPORT
LIEN

Another alternative for collecting past due child support is the use of the child support lien. Sections 157.311 through 157.326 of the Texas Family Code governs these liens, which are relatively new to Texas child support law. You can prepare one of these liens yourself. Once prepared, it is filed in the judgment records with the county clerk of any county in which the party is believed to own nonexempt real or personal property; the county in which the party who owes the child support lives; or the county in which the court of continuing jurisdiction is located.

If the party who owes the support has a case pending that would result in the receipt of money (such as an estate or as a creditor), the lien notice can be filed with the clerk of the court in which that case is pending. In that instance, you must also give a copy of the lien notice to any attorney representing the respondent in the pending lawsuit; any other individual or organization believed to be in possession of real or personal property of the parent; or any governmental unit or agency that issues or records certificates, titles, or other documents evidencing property ownership. (This means places like the car title office.)

You need to call this document a Notice of Child Support Lien. It must include the following information:

- the style, docket number, and identity of the court of this state or another state having continuing jurisdiction of the child support action;

- the name, address, and, if available, the birth date, driver's license number, social security number, of the person owing the support;

- your name and social security number and that of the children for whom support is owed;

- the amount of the child support arrearages owed and the date of the court order, administrative order, or writ that determined the amount of the arrearages or the date and manner in which the arrearages were determined;

- the rate of interest specified either in the court order or by law;

- the motor vehicle identification number shown on the obligor's title if the property you want to attach is a motor vehicle; and

- an affidavit that you have signed before a notary public.

BOND

If the parent who owes support either works for an employer who is out of state or is in a situation in which an employer's order is unworkable or inappropriate, the court can order the respondent to post a bond or other security to help insure that child support will be paid.

LICENSURE SUSPENSION

You may also get any license issued by the state and held by a parent who owes child support payments suspended. (Tex. Fam. Code, Ch. 232.) A license can be suspended if:

- there is an arrearage that is equal to or greater than the total support due for 90 days under a support order;

- the obligor has been given an opportunity to make payments toward the child support arrearage either by court order or by an agreed repayment schedule; and

- the obligor has then failed to comply with the repayment schedule.

Your petition must contain the following information:

- the name and, if known, the social security number of the party who owes the child support;

- the type and, if known, the number, of any license the person is believed to hold and the name of the licensing authority that issued the license; and

- the amount of arrearages owed under the child support order.

You should also include a copy of the official payment record.

The hearing will be conducted like the hearing for an enforcement action. Once you show that you meet the qualifications for a license suspension, the court will suspend the license unless the obligor can show either that the child support has been paid or that he proves one of the defenses to contempt.

The court can decide not to suspend the license immediately, but this will be conditioned on the obligor's compliance with a repayment schedule (which will be incorporated into the order). Once the obligor has either paid all of the delinquent child support or established a satisfactory payment record (something that will be entirely up to the judge to decide), the license suspension can be lifted by the court that ordered the suspension.

WRIT OF HABEAS CORPUS

Another remedy available, and mostly used for violations of a visitation order, is the Writ of Habeas Corpus. In order to qualify for such a writ, you must be entitled to possession of the child under a court order. The one exception to the requirement of an existing court order is if a parent is seeking the return of a child from a nonparent. And you must be entitled to possession at the time the application for the writ is presented to the court and at the time of the hearing. This remedy will not be of use with visitation violations for week-ends or short holidays. However, it is available for longer visits like the summer visitation.

In this proceeding, the person asking for the writ is called the *relator*. You will prepare an application that sets out the court order that entitles you to possession of the child and allege that you do not have possession.

The court will schedule a hearing, called a *show cause hearing*. If the court finds that you are entitled to possession of the child, the judge will order the child turned over to you at the hearing. As a part of the notice of the hearing, the party with actual possession of the child will be ordered to bring the child to court for the hearing.

You should also have an order with you at this hearing. Of course, the person who has the child has to be personally served with the notice of the application and hearing.

NOTE: *It would be best to have an attorney for this process.*

EMERGENCIES 18

On occasion, emergencies in the child custody arena do arise.

KIDNAPPING

The most extreme instance of a child custody emergency is kidnapping. There are many reasons a parent may choose to kidnap a child. They may be afraid of losing custody of the child in court, they may be concerned about abuse and neglect, or they may simply want to punish the other parent.

Regardless of the reason for hiding the child from the parent, kidnapping is a crime. If your child is kidnapped, you should notify the police. If you do not have a custody order in place, get one immediately so that it can be enforced. Also, contact the Federal Parent Locator Service. This government agency will help you try to locate the missing parent and child so that you regain possession of the child.

Once you find the other parent, you can file a certified, exemplified copy of your custody order with the court in the area in which the parent is found to assist in enforcement.

If you believe that there is a potential for kidnapping, ask the court to order supervised visits with the other parent or some other type of restriction to lower the risk that an abduction will occur. You can also ask the court to order the parent to post a bond or other security to assist in maintaining compliance with the custody and visitation provisions.

If your children are kidnapped, you should contact the police immediately. It will also be very helpful for you to consult an attorney to help you determine what court remedies may be available to you to protect your rights.

DOMESTIC VIOLENCE

If domestic violence is an issue, in addition to all of the remedies previously discussed, you should also file for a protective order. A protective order is a much better tool to use than simply a restraining order. A protective order will keep the offending party away from you, and the police will have prior notice of the order. If it is violated, the violator can be arrested immediately and charged with a criminal offense.

While you can prepare an application for a protective order yourself, there is no need for you to take on this burden. Simply contact your local District Attorney's office. They will handle this for you at no cost.

ABUSE

If you suspect that one of your children has been abused, you should always notify child protective services. The hotline for reporting abuse is 800-252-5400.

NOTE: *Failure to report suspected child abuse is a crime.*

You should also file papers in court asking the court to enter emergency orders for the protection of the children. These are the same types of orders previously discussed, and would include restricted visitation if the offender is the noncustodial parent. If the offender is the custodial parent, you would file for temporary custody as well as for permanent custody.

CHANGING COURT ORDERS 19

At some point after you have final orders for custody, support, and visitation, you may find that you need to change these orders. The person paying child support may be making more money than at the time of the original order, and the parent with primary possession will want the child support increased. Or that person may have lost a job and now be making a lot less and need the child support reduced. Perhaps the family situation for one of the parents has changed, or a child has begun having problems, and custody needs to be changed. To make the changes official, you must go back to court and ask that the order be changed. This procedure is called modification.

MODIFICATION

Modification is just like a new lawsuit, except that it is filed under the original case number. If you are filing a modification, you must either serve the respondent with *citation* or get them to sign a *waiver*. (See Chapter 4 and the glossary for more information on these terms.)

If you are responding to a modification, you must file a written answer with the court (just like in the original suit) or be subject to having a default judgment entered against you.

Modification of final orders is governed by Chapter 156 of the Texas Family Code. Under certain circumstances, custody, visitation, and child support can all be modified. These modifications must be done by the court that has continuing jurisdiction of the children; generally, this will be the court that entered the original final order. If you do not know which court has continuing jurisdiction, you can call the Bureau of Vital Statistics at 512-458-7368.)

INFORMAL AGREEMENT

Never enter into an informal agreement to modify child support or custody. Until the modification is done by court order, it is not enforceable. That means that if the person who informally gave up custody changes his or her mind at any time, he or she can demand return of the child and enforce the original order. In child support cases, you can be subject to an enforcement action on the original court ordered amount, and the court will not honor the informal agreement. If the informal agreement is for a higher amount, the court will not enforce the higher amount.

MODIFYING CUSTODY ORDERS

The rules for modification of custody orders depend on what sort of custody orders are already in place.

SOLE MANAGING CONSERVATORSHIP

If a custody order designates a sole managing conservator, the order may be modified to name a new sole managing conservator if both of the following two elements is proven:

1) the circumstances of the child, sole managing conservator, possessory conservator, or other party affected by the order have materially and substantially changed since the date of the rendition of the order, and

EVIDENCE   In a contested modification, the evidence will be basically the same as that in the standard custody case discussed in earlier chapters. However, if you are seeking the modification, you must keep in mind the statutory factors that you must prove in order to get the modification. (see pages 114 and 115.). You should tailor your evidence to those elements as much as possible so that the judge can clearly see that you have met your burden of proof on each one of the elements.

Conversely, if you are opposing a modification, you will need to make careful note of the evidence used by the other side so that if they fail to establish one of the elements, you can point that fact out to the judge with your evidence.

TEMPORARY   In a custody modification suit, the court is authorized to enter tempo-
ORDERS   rary orders to be effective while the modification is pending. (Tex. Fam. Code, Sec. 156.006.) However, in a custody modification action, this section of the Family Code places strict requirements on a temporary order that changes custody.

Other types of temporary orders are permissible (for example, for a social study, a psychological evaluation, drug testing), and the motion for the orders, the hearing, and the orders themselves work just like the temporary orders discussed earlier. However, the state policy is to minimize the disruption of the lives of children during litigation. Therefore, there are only three instances in which custody can be changed prior to the final order:

1) if the order is necessary because the child's present living environment may endanger the child's physical health or significantly impair the child's emotional development;

2) if the child's managing conservator has voluntarily relinquished actual care, control, and possession of the child for more than six months and the temporary orders are in the best interest of the child; or

3)   if the child is at least 10 years older and has signed a choice of conservator affidavit naming the person seeking the temporary order and the order is in the child's best interest.

"EMERGENCY" REQUIREMENT

By now, you have noticed that the phrase "endanger the child's physical health or significantly impair the child's emotional development" appears in some of the elements. This requirement is generally strictly interpreted by judges to cover only those situations that are very serious and genuinely constitute an emergency. If this is one of the elements you must prove, you will need something close to evidence of abuse or neglect to meet this standard. It is certainly more than just showing the court that you would be the better custodial parent and that the child would be better off with you.

MEDIATION

You may also go to mediation in a custody modification suit. The same rules and procedures previously discussed apply to modifications.

FINAL ORDER

Once you have either reached an agreement to modify custody or successfully conducted your hearing before the court, you will need to prepare a final order. Most of the provisions are just like the provisions in the original custody order. However, you will need to include findings made by the court that you have met your burden of proof on the elements required for the modification.

There are sample modification orders in the appendix for visitation and support modifications. You can adapt these forms for use in custody modification cases as well. You will need to modify the section with the findings to correspond with the elements that apply to your case and set out the appropriate new orders.

CONTESTED

Custody modification, if contested, is a significant undertaking. The courts want to encourage as much stability for the child as possible. Therefore, you should not seek to change custody just because you are angry with the child's other parent.

If you are the noncustodial parent, you should also be very careful about questioning your child about coming to live with you. Children often feel trapped in the middle of their parents in situations like this, and may feel like they have to tell you what they think you want to hear about living with them, even if they are not unhappy with the present living situation. Children also do not generally want to have to pick between parents, and this applies to modifications as well as initial custody fights.

In many instances, noncustodial parents say that their child wants to come to live with them. Then, when someone talks to the child alone, it turns out that the child does not really want to move but did not want to hurt the parent's feelings or felt pressured to say they wanted to live with that parent.

On both sides of this equation, you also need to be aware of the child who wants to live with the other parent because they believe there will be fewer rules and more freedom. This can especially be a problem with older teenagers. Before filing a modification, the noncustodial parent needs to make a realistic evaluation of what the rules for the child will be at the house and what the rules are now with the other parent. In situations like this, the grass is sometimes greener on the other side of the fence. When a child is just spending weekends with you, there is a different feel to the relationship than when you are together day in and day out.

Temporarily switching child's residence. If the parents have a good relationship, there are no significant problems, and you have an older child, you might consider a trial run living with the other parent. The risk to the custodial parent is that the child may not want to come home after living with the other party. However, many potential contested custody modifications have been stopped before they ever started by just such a trial run.

Children who have lived primarily with one parent for a period of time often want to spend more time with the other parent. Allowing this to happen can be good for the child, and can help both parents to maintain a good relationship with the child.

Homelife problems. Of course, if there are problems in one of the homes, those problems must be addressed so that the child is not adversely impacted. If you are a noncustodial parent and your child is seriously unhappy, being abused or neglected, having discipline problems, struggling in school, or having emotional problems, you should not ignore these warning signals. In that situation, you have an obligation to your child to help them get back on track.

RECENT LAW CHANGES

The 2001 legislative session made several changes to the grounds for modification of custody orders. The laws that are effective prior to September 1, 2001 made distinctions for modification grounds based on the type of conservatorship that was ordered. That meant that modification of sole managing conservatorship and joint managing conservatorship were different from each other. All of those sections were repealed in favor of a single section that was intended to apply to almost all scenarios for modifications.

Many modifications will likely be based on a showing of "material and substantial" change in the circumstances of the child or a conservator. The other possibilities for modification are that a child 12 years of age or older signs an affidavit selecting the parent with whom they want to live (see page 116) or that the conservator with primary possession voluntarily gives up primary care of the child for at least six months (see page 115). The modification under any of the three possible scenarios must still be in the best interest of the child.

MODIFYING VISITATION

The visitation portion of an order can also be modified. (Tex. Fam. Code, Secs. 145.301 through 156.304.) Generally, the party seeking the modification must prove to the court that:

- the circumstances of the child or a person affected by the order have materially and substantially changed since the rendition of the last order;

- the order has become unworkable or inappropriate under the existing circumstances;

- the notice of change of a conservator's residence required by Chapter 105 was not given;

- there was a change in a conservator's residence to a place outside the state;

- a conservator has repeatedly failed to give notice of an inability to exercise visitation; or

- a conservator of the child has had a significant history of alcohol or drug abuse since the date of the rendition of the order to be modified.

The most common of these grounds is the inappropriate or unworkable section. A sample visitation modification petition and order is included in the appendix as PETITION TO MODIFY PARENT-CHILD RELATIONSHIP (see form 24, p.236) and ORDER IN SUIT TO MODIFY PARENT-CHILD RELATIONSHIP. (see form 25, p.238.)

EVIDENCE   In determining whether or not to seek a modification under one of these sections, you need to evaluate what evidence you will have to show the court that there is a significant problem. You should not use modification litigation or the threat of such litigation simply to continue a conflict with your former spouse or to punish your former spouse. Instead, reserve modifications of visitation for situations that actually adversely affect your child. Occasionally missing visitation should not be grounds for seeking a restriction of a parent's visitation.

On the other hand, if the noncustodial parent constantly misses visitation, then shows up unexpectedly and without warning, and is really disrupting the child's life and plans, you may want to consider a modification if you and the other parent cannot resolve the problems yourselves.

MOVING THE   Another area that results in modification suits, in both the custody and vis-
CHILD   itation cases, is the instance in which one parent is moving some distance away. In many courts, there may already be an order in place that restricts the child's residence to a particular county or group of counties. If one of

the parents is going to move outside those counties, you will need to go to court if the child is going to go as well. If the child is staying, you may need to make some changes to the visitation schedule, depending on which parent is moving and on the distance that will be involved.

In a joint custody situation, courts are often very reluctant to authorize a move of the child. Therefore, if you are contemplating a move, you need to keep in mind the fact that the court may not permit you to move the child unless the other parent agrees. This can be a particular problem if you have had primary possession of the child; if the court does not authorize the child's move, you may then have to lose primary possession of the child if you follow through with your plans to move.

If one of the parents does move far enough away that increased expenses for visitation are incurred, the court can modify the orders to allocate these additional expenses. Normally, the noncustodial parent pays the costs of exercising visitation. However, the Texas Family Code establishes a rebuttable presumption that the party whose residence changes should bear the increased costs. This allocation can be made even if none of the other terms of the order are changed.

PROTECTING THE CHILD

Any time a conservator or person with court ordered access to the child is either convicted of child abuse or placed on *deferred adjudication* for a child abuse offense, the court can modify the order to protect the child. If this situation applies to your case, and you are the nonoffending party, you should file a motion to modify immediately.

This situation, and the classes of offenses that authorize a modification are set out in Section 156.304 of the Texas Family Code. Do not file a motion to modify based on this section if there has not been a conviction or deferred adjudication. If you do so, you have committed a Class B misdemeanor and are subject to criminal prosecution.

A *conviction* is self explanatory; a check of the person's criminal history will show that they have been convicted of one of these offenses. *Deferred adjudication* is slightly different. In that instance, the accused offender enters a plea, usually a no contest plea, to the charges. The court will find that the evidence substantiates their guilt but will not enter a finding or conviction, and place them on probation for a period of time. If the individual successfully completes the probation period, the case will be dismissed without the offender ever being convicted of the crime. The criminal history will show that a probation period was served, but that there was no finding of guilt. Because it is not a conviction, deferreds cannot normally be used against a party; however, this section of the Texas Family Code creates a specific instance in which it can be used.

UNIFORM CHILD CUSTODY JURISDICTION AND ENFORCEMENT ACT

If your custody or visitation order was entered in another state, then you must qualify under Chapter 152 of the Family Code, also known as the Uniform Child Custody Jurisdiction and Enforcement Act, to have a Texas court modify that order. To qualify:

- Texas must be the home state of the child on the date the modification is commenced or within six months before the commencement of the modification and the child is absent from the state but a parent or person acting as a parent continues to reside in Texas;

- a court of another state cannot be the home state of the child or the court of another state has declined to exercise jurisdiction because another state is a more appropriate and convenient forum;

- the child and at least one of the child's parents have a significant connection with Texas other than mere physical presence; or

- substantial evidence must be available in Texas concerning the child's care, protection, training, and personal relationships.

Texas can also modify an order of another state if the court of the other state finds that neither the child, the child's parents, or any person acting as a parent no longer live in that state.

MODIFYING CHILD SUPPORT

Child support can also be modified, either to increase the amount or to decrease it. Texas Family Code, Section 156.401 sets out the grounds for child support modification. The circumstances of the child or a person affected by the order must have materially and substantially changed since the rendition of the prior order. Another call for child support modification can be that it has been three years since the order was rendered or last modified, and the monthly child support amount differs from the guideline support by either 20% or by $100. If the paying parent gets a raise or suffers a long term loss of income, the support order can be modified regardless of the amount of time that has passed.

The courts will not automatically change the child support amount. The parties themselves have the burden of filing a motion to modify the child support. If you are the paying parent and have had a salary decrease or job loss that you expect to last for any length of time, you must file your modification motion right away.

The court can only retroactively modify support on payments that accrue after the earlier of the date of service of citation or an appearance (either by filing a waiver of service or an answer or coming to court for a hearing). If there is no modification suit on file, once a child support payment becomes due under the court order, there is nothing the court can do to change this amount due. You will have to pay the amount, plus interest if you are late, no matter what your financial circumstances are. A sample child support modification form, called ORDER IN SUIT TO MODIFY PARENT-CHILD RELATIONSHIP, is included in the appendix. (see form 22, p.228.)

INTENTIONAL
UNDEREMPLOYMENT

See Chapter 9, p.59 for information on how intentional underemployment affects the way courts deal with child support.

GROUNDS
NOT TO MODIFY

In a modification, support will be set based on the guidelines just like in an original support order.

There are some circumstances that the Texas Family Code specifically deems are not grounds for support modification. These are:

- a history of support voluntarily provided in excess of the court order;

- an increase in the needs, standard of living, or lifestyle of the parent receiving support since the last order; and

- remarriage.

NOTE: *The resources of a new spouse do not count in computing child support payments.*

If your child support order was rendered in another state, a Texas court can modify your order if both parents and the child reside in Texas. If you do not all reside in Texas, you will need to refer to Chapter 159 of the Texas Family Code, also known as the Uniform Interstate Family Support Act. Section 159.206 is the section that governs modification.

OTHER STATE'S
ORDER

If all parties do not live in Texas, the Texas courts can only initiate a request to the other state to modify its order unless none of the parties still reside in the original state or if they agree to allow the Texas court to assume jurisdiction. Absent an agreement or the residence of all parties in Texas, you must either file in the original state or in the state in which the responding party resides. If you are seeking a modification in a court other than the court that issued the last order, you have a duty to give notice of the new, modified order to the courts that have previously entered support orders in the case.

TERMINATION OF
PARENTAL RIGHTS

In a standard child custody setting, you can file to seek termination of the parental rights if there is child abuse or neglect, failure to support, or abandonment. (Tex. Fam. Code, Ch. 161.)

However, you should think carefully before you pursue this remedy. Terminating the relationship forever between a parent and a child is an extreme remedy, and the burden of proof is significant.

You must prove by *clear and convincing evidence* that one of the criteria for termination is met. The standard *burden of proof* in civil cases is just that it is more likely than not that the facts you allege are true (called a *preponderance of the evidence*). The familiar criminal burden of proof is *beyond a reasonable doubt*. Clear and convincing is not quite to the level of the reasonable doubt standard, but it is close.

If the termination is not going to be voluntary, you must be sure you have very strong evidence to back up your position. You need to keep in mind that filing for a termination of parental rights may entitle that parent whose rights are in jeopardy to a court appointed attorney.

NOTE: *Some parents on occasion believe that terminating their parental rights will keep them from having to pay child support. If the court believes that the only reason the termination is sought is to avoid the child support obligation, the termination request will not be approved.*

> *Warning*: Terminating a person's parental rights is an extraordinarily difficult thing to accomplish. And, if someone is trying to terminate your rights, it is a very serious matter. You should never try to handle a case of this type without the assistance of a lawyer.

Wrap-Up

You should now have a good overview of the process involved in child support, custody, and visitation cases and what to expect when you get to the courthouse. Not every situation could be covered, and there may be aspects to your case that are beyond the scope of this book, but the information provided will give you a good guide as you work your way through the legal process.

GLOSSARY

A

ad litem. An individual appointed to represent the interests of the children in a lawsuit. Also called an attorney at litem.

arrearage. An amount of unpaid child support.

associate judge. A judge who is hired by the elected district judge to hear family law matters.

attempt to marry. Legal term applied when man and woman go through a wedding ceremony, but the marriage is found to be void for some legal reason.

B

best interests. Standard used by the courts in evaluating which party should have custody.

burden of proof. The standard applied to the evidence you must have to win your case.

C

cause number.   The identifying number assigned to your case by the court.

citation.   Document prepared by the clerk to tell someone a suit has been filed against them.

conformed copy.   A copy of an order with stamp of judge's signature or a judge's signature.

community supervision.   Probation.

conservatorship.   The formal term for custody. A possessory conservator has some rights and has access to the child. A managing conservator has most or all of the rights and duties of a parent and a right to possession of the child.

contempt.   Violation of court order. Also name of procedure for asking judge to punish a party for violating a court order.

cross examination.   Questioning witnesses called to testify by another party.

custodian of records.   Person at a business or agency who works with records and can certify that copies are true and correct and made in regular course of business.

D

deferred adjudication.   Criminal sentence that involves the serving of a probation period and , upon successful completion of the probation, a dismissal of the criminal case with no finding of guilt.

deposition.   Testimony taken under oath but not in court.

direct examination.   Questioning a witness that you have called to testify.

de novo. A type of appeal hearing that involves a completely new hearing as though the first had not occurred.

due diligence. In service by publication, the effort used to locate the missing party for service of process.

E

emancipation. Time when a minor child becomes legally considered an adult.

G

guardian ad litem. Entity authorized by the court to monitor and collect child support.

H

hearsay. Something that someone told you or a document.

I

injunction-order prohibiting certain conduct. Can be the same order as a restraining order, but is done after notice to the other party and a hearing in court.

interrogatory. Discovery device involving written questions.

J

jurisdiction. Legal authority for a particular court to hear a case. Also can refer to the geographical area in which court's orders apply. Texas court orders apply all over the state. Continuing jurisdiction means that a court retains the sole authority to hear matters relating to the child after the final orders are entered.

L

leading question. A question that, by its phrasing, suggests the answer

M

motion. Document requesting a court to take a specific action or enter a specific order.

movant. Party who files a motion.

N

net resources. Amount of income to which child support guidelines are applied. Generally is total income less withholding, social security, and medicare for one dependent.

notice. Telling the other parties when and where a court proceeding is to be held.

O

obligee. Person entitled to receive child support.

obligor. Person ordered to pay child support.

P

parent. Specifically defined by the family code as mother, presumed father, a man already legally determined to be the father, an adoptive mother or father.

parentage. Also known as paternity.

paternity. Proceeding do legally establish whether a man is a child's father.

petitioner. Person who files a suit in family law cases.

pleadings. Documents filed with the court asking for action by the court.

possession (as relating to children). Having the child with you, either to live or for visitation. Possession order is the visitation schedule.

preponderance of the evidence. Standard in burden of proof meaning more likely than not.

presumed father. A man whose child is born during the marriage to the mother or within 360 days of the termination of the marriage or who marries or attempts to marry the mother after the birth of the child.

R

respondent. Person who has had suit in family court filed against them.

restraining order. Order prohibiting certain conduct. Like an injunction, but can is signed by judge without notice to the other party and without a hearing

request for admission. A statement the other party must either admit or deny.

retainer. Deposit paid to attorney to cover attorney's fees.

S

SAPCR. A suit affecting the parent-child relationship, which is a suit related to a child.

standing. The legal authority to file a suit.

social study. A report prepared by a certified social worker about the parents and the child; it includes a recommendation as to who should have custody.

style of case. The heading of the case; includes names of parties, court number, case number, and name of county.

subpoena deuces tecum. A subpoena that also requires witnesses to bring something to the proceeding.

suspended commitment. Probation period in enforcement action; allows respondent to stay out of jail as long as he meets certain conditions.

W

writ of habeas corpus. Name of proceeding and document used to order a party to bring a child to court to address violation of court orders on access.

APPENDIX
TYPICAL CASES AND SAMPLE FORMS

The following hypothetical case is a story to apply to the forms that follow it. It is a fictitious scenario of a married couple to demonstrate how the custody, visitation, and support forms would be completed based on such a case. The forms that follow are how this couple would use them. Should you decide to fill them in for yourself, you will have to retype them with your information.

TYPICAL CUSTODY CASE—CASE #1

Jane and John Smith are childhood sweethearts who got married in 1994. They are now both 27 years old and have one child, Joan, who is 6 years old. Early in 2001, John and Jane separate and John moves out. Two months pass after John moves out, and neither of them has filed for divorce. John does not pay Jane any money to help with Joan's expenses. In late March, John decides he wants custody and tells Jane that Joan must come to live with him. At the time, he seemed very angry and depressed; Joan is concerned about John's mental stability. He also tells her that he is going to take Joan out of her school and enroll her in a new one. Jane is not in agreement with this, and decides she needs to file for legal custody of Joan.

Because of John's demands and threats to take Joan out of school, Jane also decides that she needs a TEMPORARY RESTRAINING ORDER to prevent John from carrying out his plan. Therefore, Jane files for divorce from John with the ORIGINAL PETITION FOR DIVORCE (form 1) and includes in her petition the request for the restraining order. Because of her concern about his mental stability, she also asks the court to order a psychological evaluation. And, since she believes that her home is a much better place for Joan, she asks for a social study. Jane would also file are form 2 as it is required.

Before going to file, Jane also prepares the TEMPORARY RESTRAINING ORDER, form 6, leaving blanks for the date and time of the hearing in the notice.

Once she has prepared these forms, she takes them to the District Clerk of her home county, Purple County, along with her filing fee money. She tells the clerk she needs a TEMPORARY RESTRAINING ORDER and asks for citation and notice to be issued. She gets a setting from the clerk for the hearing and gets the TEMPORARY RESTRAINING ORDER signed by the judge. Since she has decided to have the constable serve the papers, she leaves them with the clerk, who will prepare the citation and notice and send the papers to the constable for service.

Purple County is fairly large, and all of the temporary hearings are heard by an Associate Judge.

When John is served with the papers, he files a RESPONDENT'S ORIGINAL ANSWER, which is found in form 7. He also files form 2, the STATEMENT ON ALTERNATIVE DISPUTE RESOLUTION. The hearing for the temporary orders is held on May 15, 2001. Jane and John each prepare FINANCIAL INFORMATION STATEMENTS (form 10) and take them to the hearing. Jane knows that Joan wants to live with her and she wants Joan to tell this to the Judge, so she files the MOTION FOR JUDGE TO CONFER (AND ORDER) (form 12).

Even though John asks for custody, by filing his own petition for divorce (now called a counter petition because he is not the original party who filed the suit), the associate judge decides that Jane should have temporary custody. The associate judge also decides to order both the social study and the psychological. John is ordered to pay child support and gets visitation according to the standard schedule.

Jane prepares the TEMPORARY ORDERS (form 14). She sends a copy to John, telling him in a letter that if he objects to the orders, he should notify the court. She sends or takes the original orders and several copies to the court clerk along with a self addressed, stamped envelope. When the judge has signed the orders, she will receive the conformed copies back from the court. She sends a signed copy to John.

While the case is pending, John gets his summer visitation with Joan. He wants to take her to Disneyworld, but the TEMPORARY ORDERS prevent him from taking Joan out of the state without the court's permission. So he files a MOTION FOR TEMPORARY ORDERS (form 5) and the NOTICE OF THE HEARING FOR TEMPORARY ORDERS (form 4). Once he has gotten the hearing set, he sends copies of both forms to Jane by certified mail. The party who wins this hearing would prepare an order reflecting the judge's decision and get it signed.

Jane decides that she needs more information from John, especially about his income and finances. He will not give her this information voluntarily, so she decides that she needs to take his deposition. She uses form 11 to give John notice of the time and place of his deposition.

Eventually, Jane and John resolve their differences and the case settles. Jane prepares the FINAL DECREE OF DIVORCE (form 8) and EMPLOYER'S ORDER TO WITHHOLD FROM EARNINGS FOR CHILD SUPPORT (form 9) and goes to court for the prove-up. The judge signs the decree, and the case is over. If John failed to file an answer after Jane had him served, Jane would prepare the final decree using the default judgment chapter for guidance and take it along with a CERTIFICATE OF LAST KNOWN ADDRESS (form 13) to the prove up.

If John and Jane reach an agreement before John has been served, he can file a WAIVER OF SERVICE (form 3) instead of being formally served by the sheriff or constable.

Table of Forms for Case #1

NO. _____

IN THE MATTER OF	§	IN THE DISTRICT COURT
THE MARRIAGE OF	§	
	§	
JANE SMITH	§	
AND	§	1ST JUDICIAL DISTRICT
JOHN SMITH	§	
	§	
AND IN THE INTEREST OF	§	
JOAN SMITH, A CHILD	§	PURPLE COUNTY, TEXAS

ORIGINAL PETITION FOR DIVORCE

I.

This suit is brought by JANE SMITH, Petitioner, who is twenty-seven (27) years of age and resides at 210 Happy Trails, Somewhere, Texas. John Smith, Respondent, is twenty-seven (27) years of age and resides at 801 Lonely Lane, Somewhere, Texas.

Petitioner has been a domiciliary of Texas for the preceding six-month period and a resident of this county for the preceding ninety-day period.

II.

Process should be served on Respondent at 801 Lonely Ln., Somewhere, Texas.

III.

No protective order under title 4 of the Texas Family Code is in effect, and no application for a protective order is pending with regard to the parties to this suit.

IV.

The parties were married on or about September 9, 1985 and ceased to live together as husband and wife on or about January 1, 2001.

The marriage has become insupportable because of discord or conflict of personalities between Petitioner and Respondent that destroys the legitimate ends of the marriage relationship and prevents any reasonable expectation of reconciliation.

V.

Petitioner and Respondent are parents of the following child of this marriage who is not under the continuing jurisdiction of any other court:

Name: Joan Smith

Sex: Female

Birthplace: Somewhere, Texas

Birth date: October 10, 1990

Present address: 210 Happy Trails, Somewhere, Texas

There are no court-ordered conservatorships, court-ordered guardianships, or other court-ordered relationships affecting the child the subject of this suit.

No property is owned or possessed by the child the subject of this suit.

Petitioner and Respondent, on final hearing, should be appointed joint managing conservators, with all the rights and duties of a parent conservator. Petitioner should have primary possession. Respondent should be ordered to make payments for the support of the child in the manner specified by the Court. Petitioner requests that the payments for the support of the child survive the death of Respondent and become the obligations of Respondent's estate.

VI.

Petitioner believes Petitioner and Respondent will enter into an agreement for the division of their estate. If such an agreement is made, Petitioner requests the Court to approve the agreement and divide their estate in a manner consistent with the agreement. If such an agreement is not made, Petitioner requests the Court to divide their estate in a manner that the Court deems just and right, as provided by law.

VII.

Discovery in this case is intended to be conducted under level 2 of rule 190 of the Texas Rules of Civil Procedure.

VII.

Petitioner requests the Court to dispense with the issuance of a bond, and Petitioner requests that Respondent be temporarily restrained immediately, without hearing, and after notice and hearing be temporarily enjoined, pending the further order of this Court, from:

1.   Communicating with Petitioner in person, by telephone, or in writing in vulgar, profane, obscene, or indecent language or in a coarse or offensive manner.

2.   Threatening Petitioner in person, by telephone, or in writing to take unlawful action against any person.

3.   Placing one or more telephone calls, anonymously, at any unreasonable hour,

in an offensive and repetitious manner, or without a legitimate purpose of communication.

    4.   Causing bodily injury to Petitioner or to a child of either party.

    5.   Threatening Petitioner or a child of either party with imminent bodily injury.

    6.   Molesting or disturbing the peace of the child or of another party.

    7.   Removing the child beyond the jurisdiction of the Court, acting directly or in concert with others.

    8.   Disrupting or withdrawing the child from the school or day-care facility where the child is presently enrolled.

    9.   Hiding or secreting the child from Petitioner or changing the child's current place of abode at 210 Happy Trails, Somewhere, Texas.

IX.

Petitioner believes that Respondent is mentally unstable and requests that the Court order Respondent to undergo a psychological evaluation. Petitioner further requests that the Court order the preparation of a social study.

X.

Petitioner has signed a statement on alternative dispute resolution, which is attached as Exhibit A.

XI.

Petitioner prays that citation and notice issue as required by law and that the Court grant a divorce and all other relief requested in this petition.

Petitioner prays that the Court immediately grant a temporary restraining order restraining Respondent, in conformity with the allegations of this petition, from the acts set forth above, and Petitioner prays that, after notice and hearing, this temporary restraining order be made a temporary injunction.

Petitioner prays for general relief.

Respectfully submitted,

_____

Jane Smith
210 Happy Trails
Somewhere, Texas 77777
555-555-1234
555-555-1239 (fax)

STATEMENT ON ALTERNATIVE DISPUTE RESOLUTION

I AM AWARE THAT IT IS THE POLICY OF THE STATE OF TEXAS TO PROMOTE THE AMICABLE AND NONJUDICIAL SETTLEMENT OF DISPUTES INVOLVING CHILDREN AND FAMILIES. I AM AWARE OF ALTERNATIVE DISPUTE RESOLUTION METHODS INCLUDING MEDIATION. WHILE I RECOGNIZE THAT ALTERNATIVE DISPUTE RESOLUTION IS AN ALTERNATIVE TO AND NOT A SUBSTITUTE FOR A TRIAL AND THAT THIS CASE MAY BE TRIED IF IT IS NOT SETTLED, I REPRESENT TO THE COURT THAT I WILL ATTEMPT IN GOOD FAITH TO RESOLVE BEFORE FINAL TRIAL CONTESTED ISSUES IN THIS CASE BY ALTERNATIVE DISPUTE RESOLUTION WITHOUT THE NECESSITY OF COURT INTERVENTION.

_____

NO. 01-1812

IN THE INTEREST OF	§	IN THE DISTRICT COURT
	§	
JOAN SMITH	§	1ST JUDICIAL DISTRICT
	§	
A CHILD	§	PURPLE COUNTY, TEXAS

WAIVER OF SERVICE

John Smith appeared in person before me today and stated under oath:

"I, John Smith, am the person named as Respondent in this case.

"I acknowledge that I have been provided a copy of the Original Petition for Divorce filed in this case. I have read and understand the contents of that document.

"I understand that the Texas Rules of Civil Procedure require, in most instances, that a party or respondent be served with citation. I do not want to be served with citation, and I waive the issuance and service of citation.

"I enter my appearance in this case for all purposes.

"I agree that this case may be taken up and considered by the Court without further notice to me.

"I agree that the case may be decided by the presiding Judge of the Court or by a duly appointed Associate Judge of the Court.

"I do not waive any rights that I may have with respect to the terms and conditions of conservatorship, support, and parental rights and duties related to the child born of my relationship with Petitioner.

"I further state that the following information is correct and that my-

Mailing address is: 801 Lonely Lane, Somewhere, Texas 77777

Telephone number is: 555-555-5555

Social Security number is: 333-33-3333

Texas driver's license number is: 12345678

"I further understand that I have a duty to notify the Court if my mailing address changes during this proceeding."

_____

John Smith

SIGNED under oath before me on _____

_____

Notary Public, State of Texas

I, the notary public whose signature appears above, certify that I am not an attorney in this case.

_____

NO. _____

IN THE MATTER OF	§	IN THE DISTRICT COURT
THE MARRIAGE OF	§	
	§	
JANE SMITH	§	
AND	§	1ST JUDICIAL DISTRICT
JOHN SMITH	§	
	§	
AND IN THE INTEREST OF	§	
JOAN SMITH, A CHILD	§	PURPLE COUNTY, TEXAS

NOTICE OF HEARING FOR TEMPORARY ORDERS

Notice is given to Respondent, John Smith, and Respondent is ORDERED to appear in person before this Court in the courthouse at Purple County Courthouse, Somewhere, Texas, on _____ at ___. m.

The child the subject of this suit is Joan Smith.

One of the purposes of the hearing is to determine whether the temporary injunction prayed for should be granted.

SIGNED on _____

_____
Judge Presiding

NO. 01-1812

IN THE MATTER OF	§	IN THE DISTRICT COURT
THE MARRIAGE OF	§	
	§	
JANE SMITH	§	
AND	§	1ST JUDICIAL DISTRICT
JOHN SMITH	§	
	§	
AND IN THE INTEREST OF	§	
JOAN SMITH, A CHILD	§	PURPLE COUNTY, TEXAS

MOTION FOR TEMPORARY ORDERS

This Motion for Temporary Orders is brought by Jane Smith, Petitioner, who shows in support:

1.   The Court has previously enjoined the parties from removing the child from the jurisdiction of the Court. Respondent would like to take the child to Disneyworld during his summer visitation period. Respondent asks that the Court enter temporary orders authorizing this trip. Petitioner has had primary possession of the child since the date of separation, and has not been receiving funds from Respondent for the support of the child. Respondent has the financial ability to pay temporary support while this case is pending for the use and benefit of their child.

Jane Smith prays that Respondent be ordered to pay guideline support for their child while this case is pending.

Jane Smith prays that the Court grant this Motion for Temporary Orders.

Respectfully submitted,

_____

Jane Smith
210 Happy Trails
Somewhere, Texas 77777
555-555-1234

SIGNED on _____.

_____

Judge or Clerk

Certificate of Service

I certify that a true copy of the above was served on all parties in accordance with the Texas Rules of Civil Procedure on April 30, 2001.

_____

NO._____

IN THE MATTER OF	§	IN THE DISTRICT COURT
THE MARRIAGE OF	§	
	§	
JANE SMITH	§	
AND	§	1ST JUDICIAL DISTRICT
JOHN SMITH	§	
	§	
AND IN THE INTEREST OF	§	
JOAN SMITH, A CHILD	§	PURPLE COUNTY, TEXAS

TEMPORARY RESTRAINING ORDER AND
ORDER SETTING HEARING FOR TEMPORARY ORDERS

The application of Petitioner for temporary restraining order was presented to the Court today.

The child the subject of this suit is Joan Smith.

The Court examined the pleadings of Petitioner and finds that Petitioner is entitled to a temporary restraining order.

IT IS THEREFORE ORDERED that the clerk of this Court issue a temporary restraining order restraining Respondent, and Respondent is immediately restrained, from:

1.	Communicating with Petitioner in person, by telephone, or in writing in vulgar, profane, obscene, or indecent language or in a coarse or offensive manner.

2.	Threatening Petitioner in person, by telephone, or in writing to take unlawful action against any person.

3.	Placing one or more telephone calls, anonymously, at any unreasonable hour, in an offensive and repetitious manner, or without a legitimate purpose of communication.

4.	Causing bodily injury to Petitioner or to a child of either party.

5.	Threatening Petitioner or a child of either party with imminent bodily injury.

6.	Molesting or disturbing the peace of the child or of another party.

7.	Removing the child beyond the jurisdiction of the Court, acting directly or in concert with others.

8.   Disrupting or withdrawing the child from the school or day-care facility where the child is presently enrolled.

9.   Hiding or secreting the child from Petitioner or changing the child's current place of abode at 210 Happy Trails, Somewhere, Texas.

This restraining order is effective immediately and shall continue in force and effect until further order of this Court or until it expires by operation of law. This order shall be binding on Respondent; on Respondent's agents, servants, and employees; and on those persons in active concert or participation with them who receive actual notice of this order by personal service or otherwise. The requirement of a bond is waived.

IT IS FURTHER ORDERED that the clerk shall issue notice to Respondent, John Smith, to appear, and Respondent is ORDERED to appear in person, before this Court in the courthouse at Purple County Courthouse, Somewhere, Texas, on _____ at ____.m. The purpose of the hearing is to determine whether, while this case is pending:

1.   The preceding temporary restraining order should be made a temporary injunction pending final hearing.

2.   Respondent should be ordered to pay child support, health insurance premiums for coverage on the child, and the child's uninsured medical expenses while this case is pending.

3.   The Court should order the preparation of a social study into the circumstances and condition of the child and of the home of any person requesting managing conservatorship or possession of the child.

4.   The Court should appoint a guardian and attorney ad litem to represent the interests of the child.

5.   The Court should make all other and further orders respecting the property and the parties that are pleaded for or that are deemed necessary and equitable and for the safety and welfare of the child.

IT IS FURTHER ORDERED that any person eighteen years of age or older who is not a party to or interested in the outcome of this case may serve any citation, notice, or process in this case.

SIGNED on _____ at ____. M.

_____
Judge Presiding

NO. 01-1812

IN THE MATTER OF	§	IN THE DISTRICT COURT
THE MARRIAGE OF	§	
	§	
JANE SMITH	§	
AND	§	1ST JUDICIAL DISTRICT
JOHN SMITH	§	
	§	
AND IN THE INTEREST OF	§	
JOAN SMITH, A CHILD	§	PURPLE COUNTY, TEXAS

RESPONDENT'S ORIGINAL ANSWER

John Smith, Respondent, files Respondent's Original Answer to Original Petition for Divorce and shows:

Respondent enters a general denial.

Respondent has signed a statement on alternative dispute resolution, which is attached as Exhibit A.

Respondent prays that Petitioner take nothing and that Respondent be granted all relief requested in this Original Answer.

Respondent prays for general relief.

Respectfully submitted,

_____

John Smith
801 Lonely Lane
Somewhere, Texas 77777
555-555-5555
555-555-5557 (fax)

Certificate of Service

I certify that a true copy of the above was served on all parties in accordance with the Texas Rules of Civil Procedure on March 30, 2001.

_____

NO. 01-1812

IN THE MATTER OF	§	IN THE DISTRICT COURT
THE MARRIAGE OF	§	
	§	
JANE SMITH	§	
AND	§	1ST JUDICIAL DISTRICT
JOHN SMITH	§	
	§	
AND IN THE INTEREST OF	§	
JOAN SMITH, A CHILD	§	PURPLE COUNTY, TEXAS

FINAL DECREE OF DIVORCE

On <u>December 31, 2001</u>, the Court heard this case.

Petitioner, Jane Smith, appeared in person and announced ready for trial.

Respondent, John Smith, appeared in person and announced ready for trial.

The record of testimony was duly reported by the court reporter for the 1st Judicial District Court.

The Court finds that the pleadings of Petitioner are in due form and contain all the allegations, information, and prerequisites required by law. The Court, after receiving evidence, finds that it has jurisdiction of this case and of all the parties and that at least sixty days have elapsed since the date the suit was filed. The Court finds that, at the time this suit was filed, Petitioner had been a domiciliary of Texas for the preceding six-month period and a resident of the county in which this suit was filed for the preceding ninety-day period. All persons entitled to citation were properly cited.

A jury was waived, and all questions of fact and of law were submitted to the Court.

The Court finds that the parties have entered into a written agreement as contained in this decree by virtue of having approved this decree as to both form and substance. To the extent permitted by law, the parties stipulate the agreement is enforceable as a contract. The Court approves the agreement of the parties as contained in this Final Decree of Divorce.

IT IS ORDERED AND DECREED that Jane Smith, Petitioner, and John Smith, Respondent, are divorced and that the marriage between them is dissolved on the ground of insupportability.

The Court finds that Petitioner and Respondent are the parents of the following child:

Name: Joan Smith

Sex: Female

Birthplace: Somewhere, Texas

Birth date: October 10, 1990

Home state: Texas

The Court finds no other children of the marriage are expected.

The Court, having considered the circumstances of the parents and of the child, finds that the following orders are in the best interest of the child.

IT IS ORDERED that Jane Smith and John Smith are appointed parent joint managing conservators of the following child: Joan Smith.

IT IS ORDERED that, at all times, Jane Smith, as a parent joint managing conservator, shall have the following rights and duty:

1.   the right to receive information from the other parent concerning the health, education, and welfare of the child;

2.   the duty to inform the other parent in a timely manner of significant information concerning the health, education, and welfare of the child;

3.   the right to confer with the other parent to the extent possible before making a decision concerning the health, education, and welfare of the child;

4.   the right of access to medical, dental, psychological, and educational records of the child;

5.   the right to consult with a physician, dentist, or psychologist of the child;

6.   the right to consult with school officials concerning the child's welfare and educational status, including school activities;

7.   the right to attend school activities;

8.   the right to be designated on the child's records as a person to be notified in case of an emergency;

9.   the right to consent to medical, dental, and surgical treatment during an emergency involving an immediate danger to the health and safety of the child; and

10. the right to manage the estate of the child to the extent the estate has been created by the parent or the parent's family.

IT IS ORDERED that, at all times, John Smith, as a parent joint managing conservator, shall have the following rights and duty:

1. the right to receive information from the other parent concerning the health, education, and welfare of the child;

2. the duty to inform the other parent in a timely manner of significant information concerning the health, education, and welfare of the child;

3. the right to confer with the other parent to the extent possible before making a decision concerning the health, education, and welfare of the child;

4. the right of access to medical, dental, psychological, and educational records of the child;

5. the right to consult with a physician, dentist, or psychologist of the child;

6. the right to consult with school officials concerning the child's welfare and educational status, including school activities;

7. the right to attend school activities;

8. the right to be designated on the child's records as a person to be notified in case of an emergency;

9. the right to consent to medical, dental, and surgical treatment during an emergency involving an immediate danger to the health and safety of the child; and

10. the right to manage the estate of the child to the extent the estate has been created by the parent or the parent's family.

IT IS ORDERED that, during her respective periods of possession, Jane Smith, as a parent joint managing conservator, shall have the following rights and duties:

1. the duty of care, control, protection, and reasonable discipline of the child;

2. the duty to support the child, including providing the child with clothing, food, shelter, and medical and dental care not involving an invasive procedure;

3. the right to consent for the child to medical and dental care not involving an invasive procedure;

4. the right to consent for the child to medical, dental, and surgical treatment

during an emergency involving immediate danger to the health and safety of the child; and

    5.   the right to direct the moral and religious training of the child.

IT IS ORDERED that, during his respective periods of possession, John Smith, as a parent joint managing conservator, shall have the following rights and duties:

    1.   the duty of care, control, protection, and reasonable discipline of the child;

    2.   the duty to support the child, including providing the child with clothing, food, shelter, and medical and dental care not involving an invasive procedure;

    3.   the right to consent for the child to medical and dental care not involving an invasive procedure;

    4.   the right to consent for the child to medical, dental, and surgical treatment during an emergency involving immediate danger to the health and safety of the child; and

    5.   the right to direct the moral and religious training of the child.

IT IS ORDERED that Jane Smith, as a parent joint managing conservator, shall have the following rights and duty:

    1.   the right to establish the primary residence of the child;

    2.   the right to consent to medical, dental, and surgical treatment involving invasive procedures and to consent to psychiatric and psychological treatment of the child;

    3.   the right to receive and give receipt for periodic payments for the support of the child and to hold or disburse these funds for the benefit of the child;

    4.   the right to represent the child in legal action and to make other decisions of substantial legal significance concerning the child;

    5.   the right to consent to marriage and to enlistment in the armed forces of the United States;

    6.   the right to make decisions concerning the child's education;

    7.   the right to the services and earnings of the child;

    8.   except when a guardian of the child's estate or a guardian or attorney ad litem has been appointed for the child, the right to act as an agent of the child in relation to the child's estate if the child's action is required by a state, the United States, or a foreign government; and

9.   the duty to manage the estate of the child to the extent the estate has been created by community property or the joint property of the parents.

Geographical Area for Primary Residence.

IT IS ORDERED that the primary residence of the child shall be Purple County, Texas. The parties shall not remove the child from Purple County, Texas for the purpose of changing the primary residence of the child until modified by further order of the court of continuing jurisdiction or by written agreement signed by the parties and filed with the court. IT IS FURTHER ORDERED that Jane Smith shall have the exclusive right to establish the child's primary residence within Purple County, Texas.

IT IS ORDERED that each parent shall have the duty to inform the other parent if the parent resides with for at least 30 days, marries, or intends to marry a person who the parent knows: 1) is registered as a sex offender under Chapter 62, Code of Criminal Procedure; or 2) is currently charged with an offense for which on conviction the person would be required to register under that chapter. This notice shall be made as soon as practicable but not later than the 40th day after the date the parent begins to reside with the person or the 10th day after the date the marriage occurs, as appropriate. The notice must include a description of the offense that is the basis of the person's requirement to register as a sex offender or of the offense with which the person is charged.

Standard Possession Order

The Court finds that the following provisions of this Standard Possession Order are intended to and do comply with the requirements of Texas Family Code sections 153.311 through 153.317. IT IS ORDERED that the conservators shall comply with all terms and conditions of this Standard Possession Order. IT IS ORDERED that this Standard Possession Order is effective immediately and applies to all periods of possession occurring on and after the signing of this Standard Possession Order. IT IS, THEREFORE, ORDERED:

(a)   Definitions

1.   In this Standard Possession Order "school" means the primary or secondary school in which the child is enrolled or, if the child is not enrolled in a primary or secondary school, the public school district in which the child primarily resides.

2.   In this Standard Possession Order "child" includes each child, whether one or more, who is a subject of this suit while that child is under the age of eighteen years and not otherwise emancipated.

(b)   Mutual Agreement or Specified Terms for Possession

IT IS ORDERED that the conservators shall have possession of the child at times mutually agreed to in advance by the parties, and, in the absence of mutual agreement, it is ORDERED that the conservators shall have possession of the child under the specified terms set out in this Standard Possession Order.

(c)   Parents Who Reside 100 Miles or Less Apart

Except as otherwise explicitly provided in this Standard Possession Order, when John Smith resides 100 miles or less from the primary residence of the child, John Smith shall have the right to possession of the child as follows:

1.   Weekends - On weekends, beginning at the time the child's school is regularly dismissed, on the first, third, and fifth Friday of each month and ending at the time the child's school resumes after the weekend.

2.   Weekend Possession Extended by a Holiday - Except as otherwise explicitly provided in this Standard Possession Order, if a weekend period of possession by John Smith begins on a Friday that is a school holiday during the regular school term or a federal, state, or local holiday during the summer months when school is not in session, or if the period ends on or is immediately followed by a Monday that is such a holiday, that weekend period of possession shall begin at the time the child's school is regularly dismissed on the Thursday immediately preceding the Friday holiday or school holiday or end at the time school resumes after that holiday, as applicable.

3.   Wednesdays - On Wednesday of each week during the regular school term, beginning at the time the child's school is regularly dismissed and ending at the time the child's school resumes on Thursday.

4.   Christmas Holidays in Even-Numbered Years - In even-numbered years, beginning at the time the child's school is regularly dismissed on the day the child is dismissed from school for the Christmas school vacation and ending at noon on December 26.

5.   Christmas Holidays in Odd-Numbered Years - In odd-numbered years, beginning at noon on December 26 and ending at the time the child's school resumes after that Christmas school vacation.

6.   Thanksgiving in Odd-Numbered Years - In odd-numbered years, beginning at the time the child's school is regularly dismissed on the day the child is dismissed from school for the Thanksgiving holiday and ending at the time the child's school resumes after that Thanksgiving holiday.

7.   Spring Break in Even-Numbered Years - In even-numbered years, beginning at

the time the child's school is regularly dismissed on the day the child is dismissed from school for the school's spring vacation and ending at the time school resumes after that vacation.

8.   Extended Summer Possession by John Smith

With Written Notice by April 1 - If John Smith gives Jane Smith written notice by April 1 of a year specifying an extended period or periods of summer possession for that year, John Smith shall have possession of the child for thirty days beginning no earlier than the day after the child's school is dismissed for the summer vacation and ending no later than seven days before school resumes at the end of the summer vacation in that year, to be exercised in no more than two separate periods of at least seven consecutive days each, as specified in the written notice. These periods of possession shall begin and end at 6:00 p.m.

Without Written Notice by April 1 - If John Smith does not give Jane Smith written notice by April 1 of a year specifying an extended period or periods of summer possession for that year, John Smith shall have possession of the child for thirty consecutive days in that year beginning at 6:00 p.m. on July 1 and ending at 6:00 p.m. on July 31.

9.   Child's Birthday - If John Smith is not otherwise entitled under this Standard Possession Order to present possession of the child on the child's birthday, John Smith shall have possession of the child beginning at 6:00 p.m. and ending at 8:00 p.m. on that day, provided that John Smith picks up the child from Jane Smith's residence and returns the child to that same place.

10.   Father's Day Weekend - Each year, beginning at 6:00 p.m. on the Friday preceding Father's Day and ending at 6:00 p.m. on Father's Day, provided that if he is not otherwise entitled under this Standard Possession Order to present possession of the child, he shall pick up the child from Jane Smith's residence and return the child to that same place.

Notwithstanding the weekend and Wednesday periods of possession ORDERED for John Smith, it is explicitly ORDERED that Jane Smith shall have a superior right of possession of the child as follows:

1.   Christmas Holidays in Odd-Numbered Years - In odd-numbered years, beginning at 6:00 p.m. on the day the child is dismissed from school for the Christmas school vacation and ending at noon on December 26.

2.   Christmas Holidays in Even-Numbered Years - In even-numbered years, beginning at noon on December 26 and ending at 6:00 p.m. on the day before school resumes after that Christmas school vacation.

3.   Thanksgiving in Even-Numbered Years - In even-numbered years, beginning at 6:00 p.m. on the day the child is dismissed from school for the Thanksgiving holiday and ending at 6:00 p.m. on the following Sunday.

4.   Spring Break in Odd-Numbered Years - In odd-numbered years, beginning at 6:00 p.m. on the day the child is dismissed from school for the school's spring vacation and ending at 6:00 p.m. on the day before school resumes after that vacation.

5.   Summer Weekend Possession by Jane Smith - If Jane Smith gives John Smith written notice by April 15 of a year, Jane Smith shall have possession of the child on any one weekend beginning at 6:00 p.m. on Friday and ending at 6:00 p.m. on the following Sunday during any one period of the extended summer possession by John Smith in that year, provided that Jane Smith picks up the child from John Smith and returns the child to that same place.

6.   Extended Summer Possession by Jane Smith - If Jane Smith gives John Smith written notice by April 15 of a year or gives John Smith fourteen days' written notice on or after April 16 of a year, Jane Smith may designate one weekend beginning no earlier than the day after the child's school is dismissed for the summer vacation and ending no later than seven days before school resumes at the end of the summer vacation, during which an otherwise scheduled weekend period of possession by John Smith shall not take place in that year, provided that the weekend so designated does not interfere with John Smith's period or periods of extended summer possession or with Father's Day Weekend.

7.   Child's Birthday - If Jane Smith is not otherwise entitled under this Standard Possession Order to present possession of the child on the child's birthday, Jane Smith shall have possession of the child beginning at 6:00 p.m. and ending at 8:00 p.m. on that day, provided that Jane Smith picks up the child from John Smith's residence and returns the child to that same place.

8.   Mother's Day Weekend - Each year, beginning at 6:00 p.m. on the Friday preceding Mother's Day and ending at 6:00 p.m. on Mother's Day, provided that if Jane Smith is not otherwise entitled under this Standard Possession Order to present possession of the child, she shall pick up the child from John Smith's residence and return the child to that same place.

Jane Smith shall have the right of possession of the child at all other times not specifically designated in this Standard Possession Order for John Smith.

(d)   Parents Who Reside More Than 100 Miles Apart

Except as otherwise explicitly provided in this Standard Possession Order, when John Smith resides more than 100 miles from the residence of the child, John Smith shall have the right to possession of the child as follows:

1.   Weekends - Unless John Smith elects the alternative period of weekend possession described in the next paragraph, John Smith shall have the right to possession of the child on weekends, beginning at the time the child's school is regularly dismissed on the first, third, and fifth Friday of each month and ending at the time the child's school resumes after the weekend. Except as otherwise explicitly provided in this Standard Possession Order, if such a weekend period of possession by John Smith begins on a Friday that is a school holiday during the regular school term or a federal, state, or local holiday during the summer months when school is not in session, or if the period ends on or is immediately followed by a Monday that is such a holiday, that weekend period of possession shall begin at the time the child's school is regularly dismissed on the Thursday immediately preceding the Friday holiday or school holiday or end at the time school resumes after that holiday, as applicable.

Alternate weekend possession - In lieu of the weekend possession described in the foregoing paragraph, John Smith shall have the right to possession of the child not more than one weekend per month of John Smith's choice beginning at the time the child's school is regularly dismissed on the day school recesses for the weekend and ending at the time school resumes after the weekend. Except as otherwise explicitly provided in this Standard Possession Order, if such a weekend period of possession by John Smith begins on a Friday that is a school holiday during the regular school term or a federal, state, or local holiday during the summer months when school is not in session, or if the period ends on or is immediately followed by a Monday that is such a holiday, that weekend period of possession shall begin at the time the child's school is regularly dismissed on the Thursday immediately preceding the Friday holiday or school holiday or end at the time school resumes after that holiday, as applicable. John Smith may elect an option for this alternative period of weekend possession by giving written notice to Jane Smith within ninety days after the parties begin to reside more than 100 miles apart. If John Smith makes this election, John Smith shall give Jane Smith fourteen days' written or telephonic notice preceding a designated weekend. The weekends chosen shall not conflict with the provisions regarding Christmas, Thanksgiving, the child's birthday, and Mother's Day Weekend below.

2.   Christmas Holidays in Even-Numbered Years - In even-numbered years, beginning at the time the child's school is regularly dismissed on the day the child is dismissed from school for the Christmas school vacation and ending at noon on December 26.

3.   Christmas Holidays in Odd-Numbered Years - In odd-numbered years, beginning at noon on December 26 and ending at the time the child's school resumes after that Christmas school vacation.

4.   Thanksgiving in Odd-Numbered Years - In odd-numbered years, beginning at the time the child's school is regularly dismissed on the day the child is dismissed from school for the Thanksgiving holiday and ending at the time the child's school resumes after that Thanksgiving holiday.

5.   Spring Break in All Years - Every year, beginning at the time the child's school is regularly dismissed on the day the child is dismissed from school for the school's spring vacation and ending at the time school resumes after that vacation.

6.   Extended Summer Possession by John Smith -

With Written Notice by April 1 - If John Smith gives Jane Smith written notice by April 1 of a year specifying an extended period or periods of summer possession for that year, John Smith shall have possession of the child for forty-two days beginning no earlier than the day after the child's school is dismissed for the summer vacation and ending no later than seven days before school resumes at the end of the summer vacation in that year, to be exercised in no more than two separate periods of at least seven consecutive days each, as specified in the written notice. These periods of possession shall begin and end at 6:00 p.m.

Without Written Notice by April 1 - If John Smith does not give Jane Smith written notice by April 1 of a year specifying an extended period or periods of summer possession for that year, John Smith shall have possession of the child for forty-two consecutive days beginning at 6:00 p.m. on June 15 and ending at 6:00 p.m. on July 27 of that year.

7.   Child's Birthday - If John Smith is not otherwise entitled under this Standard Possession Order to present possession of the child on the child's birthday, John Smith shall have possession of the child beginning at 6:00 p.m. and ending at 8:00 p.m. on that day, provided that John Smith picks up the child from Jane Smith's residence and returns the child to that same place.

8.   Father's Day Weekend - Each year, beginning at 6:00 p.m. on the Friday preceding Father's Day and ending at 6:00 p.m. on Father's Day, provided that if John Smith is not otherwise entitled under this Standard Possession Order to present possession of the child, he shall pick up the child from Jane Smith's residence and return the child to that same place.

Notwithstanding the weekend periods of possession ORDERED for John Smith, it is explicitly ORDERED that Jane Smith shall have a superior right of possession of the child as follows:

1.   Christmas Holidays in Odd-Numbered Years - In odd-numbered years, beginning at 6:00 p.m. on the day the child is dismissed from school for the Christmas school vacation and ending at noon on December 26.

2.   Christmas Holidays in Even-Numbered Years - In even-numbered years, beginning at noon on December 26 and ending at 6:00 p.m. on the day before school resumes after that Christmas school vacation.

3.   Thanksgiving in Even-Numbered Years - In even-numbered years, beginning at 6:00 p.m. on the day the child is dismissed from school for the Thanksgiving holiday and ending at 6:00 p.m. on the following Sunday.

4.   Summer Weekend Possession by Jane Smith - If Jane Smith gives John Smith written notice by April 15 of a year, Jane Smith shall have possession of the child on any one weekend beginning at 6:00 p.m. on Friday and ending at 6:00 p.m. on the following Sunday during any one period of possession by John Smith during John Smith's extended summer possession in that year, provided that if a period of possession by John Smith in that year exceeds thirty days, Jane Smith may have possession of the child under the terms of this provision on any two nonconsecutive weekends during that period and provided that Jane Smith picks up the child from John Smith and returns the child to that same place.

5.   Extended Summer Possession by Jane Smith - If Jane Smith gives John Smith written notice by April 15 of a year, Jane Smith may designate twenty-one days beginning no earlier than the day after the child's school is dismissed for the summer vacation and ending no later than seven days before school resumes at the end of the summer vacation in that year, to be exercised in no more than two separate periods of at least seven consecutive days each, during which John Smith shall not have possession of the child, provided that the period or periods so designated do not interfere with John Smith's period or periods of extended summer possession or with Father's Day Weekend.

6.   Child's Birthday - If Jane Smith is not otherwise entitled under this Standard Possession Order to present possession of the child on the child's birthday, Jane Smith shall have possession of the child beginning at 6:00 p.m. and ending at 8:00 p.m. on that day, provided that Jane Smith picks up the child from John Smith's residence and returns the child to that same place.

7.   Mother's Day Weekend - Each year, beginning at 6:00 p.m. on the Friday preceding Mother's Day and ending at 6:00 p.m. on Mother's Day, provided that if Jane Smith

is not otherwise entitled under this Standard Possession Order to present possession of the child, she shall pick up the child from John Smith's residence and return the child to that same place.

Jane Smith shall have the right of possession of the child at all other times not specifically designated in this Standard Possession Order for John Smith.

(e)   General Terms and Conditions

Except as otherwise explicitly provided in this Standard Possession Order, the terms and conditions of possession of the child that apply regardless of the distance between the residence of a parent and the child are as follows:

1.   Surrender of Child by Jane Smith - Jane Smith is ORDERED to surrender the child to John Smith at the beginning of each period of John Smith's possession at the residence of Jane Smith.

If a period of possession by John Smith begins at the time the child's school is regularly dismissed, Jane Smith is ORDERED to surrender the child to John Smith at the beginning of each such period of possession at the school in which the child is enrolled. If the child is not in school, John Smith shall pick up the child at the residence of Jane Smith at 210 Happy Trails, Somewhere, Texas, and Jane Smith is ORDERED to surrender the child to John Smith at the residence of Jane Smith at 210 Happy Trails, Somewhere, Texas under these circumstances.

2.   Return of Child by John Smith - John Smith is ORDERED to return the child to the residence of Jane Smith at the end of each period of possession. However, it is ORDERED that, if Jane Smith and John Smith live in the same county at the time of rendition of this order, John Smith's county of residence remains the same after rendition of this order, and Jane Smith's county of residence changes, effective on the date of the change of residence by Jane Smith, John Smith shall surrender the child to Jane Smith at the residence of John Smith at the end of each period of possession.

If a period of possession by John Smith ends at the time the child's school resumes, John Smith is ORDERED to surrender the child to Jane Smith at the end of each period of possession at the school in which the child is enrolled or, if the child is not in school, at the residence of Jane Smith at 210 Happy Trails, Somewhere, Texas.

3.   Surrender of Child by John Smith - John Smith is ORDERED to surrender the child to Jane Smith, if the child is in John Smith's possession or subject to John Smith's control, at the beginning of each period of Jane Smith's exclusive periods of possession, at the

place designated in this Standard Possession Order.

4.   Return of Child by Jane Smith - Jane Smith is ORDERED to return the child to John Smith, if John Smith is entitled to possession of the child, at the end of each of Jane Smith's exclusive periods of possession, at the place designated in this Standard Possession Order.

5.   Personal Effects - Each conservator is ORDERED to return with the child the personal effects that the child brought at the beginning of the period of possession.

6.   Designation of Competent Adult - Each conservator may designate any competent adult to pick up and return the child, as applicable. IT IS ORDERED that a conservator or a designated competent adult be present when the child is picked up or returned.

7.   Inability to Exercise Possession - Each conservator is ORDERED to give notice to the person in possession of the child on each occasion that the conservator will be unable to exercise that conservator's right of possession for any specified period.

8.   Written Notice - Written notice shall be deemed to have been timely made if received or postmarked before or at the time that notice is due.

9.   Notice to School and Jane Smith - If John Smith's time of possession of the child ends at the time school resumes and for any reason the child is not or will not be returned to school, John Smith shall immediately notify the school and Jane Smith that the child will not be or has not been returned to school.

This concludes the Standard Possession Order.

Duration.

The periods of possession ordered above apply to the child the subject of this suit while that child is under the age of eighteen years and not otherwise emancipated.

Mediation of Future Disputes. Note: This clause is not required.

IT IS ORDERED that before any party files suit for modification of the terms and conditions of conservatorship, possession, or support of the child, except in an emergency, that party shall attempt to mediate in good faith the controversy as provided in chapter 153 of the Texas Family Code. This requirement does not apply to actions brought to enforce this Final Decree of Divorce.

Child Support.

IT IS ORDERED that John Smith is obligated to pay and shall pay to Jane Smith child support of $500 per month, with the first payment being due and payable on January 1, 2002 and a like payment being due and payable on the first day of each month thereafter until the first month following the date of the earliest occurrence of one of the events specified below:

1.   the child reaches the age of eighteen years, provided that, if the child is fully enrolled in an accredited secondary school in a program leading toward a high school diploma or enrolled in courses for joint high school and junior college credit pursuant to Section 130.008, Education Code, the periodic child-support payments shall continue to be due and paid until the end of the month in which the child graduates from high school;

2.   the child marries;

3.   the child dies;

4.   the child's disabilities are otherwise removed for general purposes; or

5.   further order modifying this child support.

Withholding from Earnings.

IT IS ORDERED that any employer of John Smith shall be ordered to withhold from earnings for child support from the disposable earnings of John Smith for the support of Joan Smith.

IT IS ORDERED that all payments shall be made through the Purple County Child Support Office, Purple County Courthouse, Somewhere, Texas 77777 and then remitted by that agency to Jane Smith for the support of the child. IT IS FURTHER ORDERED that John Smith shall pay, when due, all fees charged by that agency.

IT IS FURTHER ORDERED that John Smith shall notify this Court and Jane Smith by U.S. certified mail, return receipt requested, of any change of address and of any termination of employment. This notice shall be given no later than seven days after the change of address or the termination of employment. This notice or a subsequent notice shall also provide the current address of John Smith and the name and address of obligor's current employer, whenever that information becomes available.

IT IS ORDERED that, on the request of a prosecuting attorney, the attorney general, the friend of the Court, Jane Smith, or John Smith, the clerk of this Court shall cause a certified copy of the "Employer's Order to Withhold from Earnings for Child Support" to be delivered to any employer. IT IS FURTHER ORDERED that the clerk of this Court shall attach a copy of subchapter C of chapter 158 of the Texas Family Code for the information of any employer.

Health Care.

IT IS ORDERED that medical support shall be provided for the child as follows:

IT IS ORDERED that, as additional child support, John Smith shall provide health insurance for the parties' child, for as long as child support is payable under the terms of this decree, as set out herein.

"Health insurance" means insurance coverage that provides basic health-care services, including usual physician services, office visits, hospitalization, and laboratory, X-ray, and emergency services, and may be provided in the form of an indemnity insurance contract or plan, a preferred provider organization or plan, a health maintenance organization, or any combination thereof.

IT IS ORDERED that John Smith shall at his sole cost and expense, keep and maintain at all times in full force and effect the health insurance coverage that insures the parties' child through John Smith's employer, union, trade association, or other organization for as long as it is offered by his employer, union, trade association, or other organization. If his employer, union, trade association, or other organization subsequently changes health insurance benefits or carriers, John Smith is ORDERED to obtain and maintain coverage for the benefit of the child on the successor company or through such health insurance plan as is available through other employment, union, trade association, or other organization or other insurance provider.

IT IS ORDERED that if John Smith is leaving that employment, union, trade association, or other organization or for any other reason health insurance will not be available for the child through the employment or membership in a union, trade association, or other organization of either party, John Smith shall within ten days of termination of his or her employment or coverage, convert the policy to individual coverage for the child in an amount equal to or exceeding the coverage at the time his or her employment or coverage is terminated. Alternatively, if that health insurance was available through Jane Smith's employment or membership in a union, trade association, or other organization, John Smith shall reimburse Jane Smith for the cost of the converted policy as follows: John Smith is ORDERED to pay to Jane Smith at her last known address the cost of insuring the child under the converted policy, on the first day of each month after John Smith receives written notice of the premium from Jane Smith for payment. Accompanying the first such written notification and any subsequent notifications informing of a change in the premium amount, Jane Smith is ORDERED to provide John Smith with documentation from the carrier of the cost to Jane Smith of providing coverage for the child.

If Policy Not Convertible - If the health insurance policy covering the child is not convertible and if no health insurance is available for the child through the employment or membership in a union, trade association, or other organization of either party, IT IS ORDERED that John Smith shall purchase and maintain, at his sole cost and expense, health insurance coverage for the child Joan Smith. John Smith is ORDERED to provide verification of the purchase of the insurance to Jane Smith at Jane Smith's last known address, including the insurance certificate number and the plan summary, no later than fifteen days following the issuance of the policy.

Except as provided in paragraph 13 below, the party who is not carrying the health insurance policy covering the child is ORDERED to submit to the party carrying the policy, within ten days of receiving them, any and all forms, receipts, bills, and statements reflecting the health-care expenses the party not carrying the policy incurs on behalf of the child.

The party who is carrying the health insurance policy covering the child is ORDERED to submit all forms required by the insurance company for payment or reimbursement of health-care expenses incurred by either party on behalf of the child to the insurance carrier within ten days of that party's receiving any form, receipt, bill, or statement reflecting the expenses.

Constructive Trust for Payments Received - IT IS ORDERED that any insurance payments received by the party carrying the health insurance policy covering the child from the health insurance carrier as reimbursement for health-care expenses incurred by or on behalf of the child shall belong to the party who incurred and paid those expenses. IT IS FURTHER ORDERED that the party carrying the policy is designated a constructive trustee to receive any insurance checks or payments for health-care expenses incurred and paid by the other party, and the party carrying the policy shall endorse and forward the checks or payments, along with any explanation of benefits, to the other party within three days of receiving them.

Filing by Party Not Carrying Insurance - In accordance with article 3.51-13 of the Texas Insurance Code, IT IS ORDERED that the party who is not carrying the health insurance policy covering the child may, at that party's option, file directly with the insurance carrier with whom coverage is provided for the benefit of the child any claims for health-care expenses, including, but not limited to, medical, hospitalization, and dental costs.

Secondary Coverage - IT IS ORDERED that nothing in this decree shall prevent either party from providing secondary health insurance coverage for the child at that party's sole cost and expense. IT IS FURTHER ORDERED that if a party provides secondary health insurance coverage for the child, both parties shall cooperate fully with regard to the handling and filing of claims with the insurance carrier providing the coverage in order to maximize the benefits available to the child and to ensure that the party who pays for health-care expenses for the child is reimbursed for the payment from both carriers to the fullest extent possible.

Compliance with Insurance Company Requirements - Each party is ORDERED to conform to all requirements imposed by the terms and conditions of the policy of health insurance covering the child in order to assure maximum reimbursement or direct payment by the insurance company of the incurred health-care expense, including but not limited to requirements for advance notice to carrier, second opinions, and the like. Each party is ORDERED to attempt to use "preferred providers," or services within the health maintenance organization, if applicable; however, this provision shall not apply if emergency care is required. Disallowance of the bill by a health insurer shall not excuse the obligation of either party to make payment; however, if a bill is disallowed or the benefit reduced due to the failure of a party to follow procedures or requirements of the carrier, including the failure of a party to use a permitted provider in other than an emergency, that party shall be wholly responsible for the increased portion of that bill.

Except as provided above, each party is ORDERED to pay 50 percent of all reasonable and necessary health-care expenses not paid by insurance and incurred by or on behalf of the parties' child, including, without limitation, any copayments for office visits or prescription drugs, the yearly deductible, if any, and medical, surgical, prescription drug, mental health-care services, dental, eye care, ophthalmological, and orthodontic charges, for as long as child support is payable under the terms of this decree.

Exclusions - The provisions above concerning uninsured expenses shall not be interpreted to include expenses for travel to and from the health-care provider or nonprescription medication.

Reasonableness of Charges - IT IS ORDERED that reasonableness of the charges for health-care expenses shall be presumed on presentation of the bill to a party and that disallowance of the bill by a health insurer shall not excuse that party's obligation to make payment or reimbursement as otherwise provided herein.

Information Required - IT IS ORDERED that a party providing health insurance shall furnish to the other party the following information no later than the thirtieth day after the date the notice of the rendition of this decree is received:

(a)   the Social Security number of the party providing insurance;

(b)   the name and address of the employer of the party providing insurance;

(c)   whether the employer is self-insured or has health insurance available;

(d)   proof that health insurance has been provided for the child; and

(e)   the name of the health insurance carrier, the number of the policy, a copy of the policy and schedule of benefits, a health insurance membership card, claim forms, and any other information necessary to submit a claim or, if the employer is self-insured, a copy of the schedule of benefits, a membership card, claim forms, and any other information necessary to submit a claim.

IT IS FURTHER ORDERED that any party carrying health insurance on the child shall furnish to the other party a copy of any renewals or changes to the policy no later than the fifteenth day after the renewal or change is received.

Termination or Lapse of Insurance - If the health insurance coverage for the child lapses or terminates, the party who is providing the insurance is ORDERED to notify the other party no later than the fifteenth day after the date of termination or lapse. If additional health insurance is available or becomes available to John Smith for the child, John Smith must notify Jane Smith no later than the fifteenth day after the date the insurance becomes available. John Smith must enroll the child in a health insurance plan at the next available enrollment period.

WARNING - A PARENT ORDERED TO PROVIDE HEALTH INSURANCE WHO FAILS TO DO SO IS LIABLE FOR NECESSARY MEDICAL EXPENSES OF THE CHILD, WITHOUT REGARD TO WHETHER THE EXPENSES WOULD HAVE BEEN PAID IF HEALTH INSURANCE HAD BEEN PROVIDED.

No Credit for Informal Payments.

IT IS ORDERED that the child support as prescribed in this decree shall be exclusively discharged in the manner ordered and that any direct payments made by John Smith to Jane Smith or any expenditures incurred by John Smith during John Smith's periods of possession of or access to the child, as prescribed in this decree, for food, clothing, gifts, travel, shelter, or entertainment are deemed in addition to and not in lieu of the support ordered in this decree.

Support as Obligation of Estate.

IT IS ORDERED that the provisions for child support in this decree shall be an obligation of the estate of John Smith and shall not terminate on the death of John Smith. Payments received for the benefit of the child from the Social Security Administration, Department of Veterans Affairs, other government agency, or life insurance shall be a credit against this obligation.

Medical Notification.

Each party is ORDERED to inform the other party within twenty-four hours of any medical condition of the parties' child requiring surgical intervention, hospitalization, or both.

Information Regarding Parties and Child

The information required for each party by section 105.006(a) of the Texas Family Code is as follows:

Name: Jane Smith

Social Security number: 999-99-9999

Driver's license number: 87654321   Issuing state: Texas

Current residence address: 210 Happy Trails, Somewhere, Texas 77777

Mailing address: 210 Happy Trails, Somewhere, Texas 77777

Home telephone number: 555-5551234

Name of employer: Somewhere School District

Address of employment: 222 Learning Way, Somewhere, Texas 77777

Work telephone number: 555-555-0000

Name: John Smith

Social Security number: 888-88-8888

Driver's license number   12345678   Issuing state: Texas

Current residence address: 801 Lonely Lane, Somewhere, Texas 77777

Mailing address: 801 Lonely Lane, Somewhere, Texas 77777

Home telephone number: 555-555-5555

Name of employer: Big Company, Inc.

Address of employment: 234 Big Company Way, Somewhere, Texas 77777

Work telephone number: 555-555-9999

Name: Joan Smith

Social Security number: 777-77-7777

Driver's license number: none   Issuing state: Texas

Current residence address: with Petitioner

Mailing address: same

Home telephone number: 555-555-1234

Name of employer: none

Address of employment: none

Work telephone number: none

EACH PERSON WHO IS A PARTY TO THIS ORDER IS ORDERED TO NOTIFY EACH OTHER PARTY, THE COURT, AND THE STATE CASE REGISTRY OF ANY CHANGE IN THE PARTY'S CURRENT RESIDENCE ADDRESS, MAILING ADDRESS, HOME TELEPHONE NUMBER, NAME OF EMPLOYER, ADDRESS OF EMPLOYMENT, DRIVER'S LICENSE NUMBER, AND WORK TELEPHONE NUMBER. THE PARTY IS ORDERED TO GIVE NOTICE OF AN INTENDED CHANGE IN ANY OF THE REQUIRED INFORMATION TO EACH OTHER PARTY, THE COURT, AND THE STATE CASE REGISTRY ON OR BEFORE THE 60TH DAY BEFORE THE INTENDED CHANGE. IF THE PARTY DOES NOT KNOW OR COULD NOT HAVE KNOWN OF THE CHANGE IN SUFFICIENT TIME TO PROVIDE 60-DAY NOTICE, THE PARTY IS ORDERED TO GIVE NOTICE OF THE CHANGE ON OR BEFORE THE FIFTH DAY AFTER THE DATE THAT THE PARTY KNOWS OF THE CHANGE.

THE DUTY TO FURNISH THIS INFORMATION TO EACH OTHER PARTY, THE COURT, AND THE STATE CASE REGISTRY CONTINUES AS LONG AS ANY PERSON, BY VIRTUE OF THIS ORDER, IS UNDER AN OBLIGATION TO PAY CHILD SUPPORT OR ENTITLED TO POSSESSION OF OR ACCESS TO A CHILD.

FAILURE BY A PARTY TO OBEY THE ORDER OF THIS COURT TO PROVIDE EACH OTHER PARTY, THE COURT, AND THE STATE CASE REGISTRY WITH THE CHANGE IN THE REQUIRED INFORMATION MAY RESULT IN FURTHER LITIGATION TO ENFORCE THE ORDER, INCLUDING CONTEMPT OF COURT. A FINDING OF CONTEMPT MAY BE PUNISHED BY CONFINEMENT IN JAIL FOR UP TO SIX MONTHS, A FINE OF UP TO $500 FOR EACH VIOLATION, AND A MONEY JUDGMENT FOR PAYMENT OF ATTORNEY'S FEES AND COURT COSTS.

Notice shall be given to the other party by delivering a copy of the notice to the party by registered or certified mail, return receipt requested. Notice shall be given to the Court by delivering a copy of the notice either in person to the clerk of the Court or by registered or certified mail addressed to the clerk. Notice shall be given to the state case registry by mailing a copy of the notice to State Case Registry, Central File Maintenance, P.O. Box 12048, Austin, Texas 78711-2048.

WARNINGS TO PARTIES: FAILURE TO OBEY A COURT ORDER FOR CHILD SUPPORT OR FOR POSSESSION OF OR ACCESS TO A CHILD MAY RESULT IN FURTHER LITIGATION TO ENFORCE THE ORDER, INCLUDING CONTEMPT OF

COURT. A FINDING OF CONTEMPT MAY BE PUNISHED BY CONFINEMENT IN JAIL FOR UP TO SIX MONTHS, A FINE OF UP TO $500 FOR EACH VIOLATION, AND A MONEY JUDGMENT FOR PAYMENT OF ATTORNEY'S FEES AND COURT COSTS.

FAILURE OF A PARTY TO MAKE A CHILD SUPPORT PAYMENT TO THE PLACE AND IN THE MANNER REQUIRED BY A COURT ORDER MAY RESULT IN THE PARTY'S NOT RECEIVING CREDIT FOR MAKING THE PAYMENT.

FAILURE OF A PARTY TO PAY CHILD SUPPORT DOES NOT JUSTIFY DENY-ING THAT PARTY COURT-ORDERED POSSESSION OF OR ACCESS TO A CHILD. REFUSAL BY A PARTY TO ALLOW POSSESSION OF OR ACCESS TO A CHILD DOES NOT JUSTIFY FAILURE TO PAY COURT-ORDERED CHILD SUPPORT TO THAT PARTY.

The Court ORDERS that the property of the parties be awarded

to the person in possession of it.

IT IS ORDERED AND DECREED that costs of court are to be borne by the party who incurred them.

IT IS ORDERED AND DECREED that the parties are discharged from the require-ment of keeping and storing the documents produced in this case in accordance with rule 191.4(d) of the Texas Rules of Civil Procedure.

Without affecting the finality of this Final Decree of Divorce, this Court expressly reserves the right to make orders necessary to clarify and enforce this decree.

IT IS ORDERED AND DECREED that all relief requested in this case and not expressly granted is denied.

SIGNED on _____.

_____
JUDGE PRESIDING

APPROVED AND CONSENTED TO
AS TO BOTH FORM AND SUBSTANCE:

_____

_____

NO. 01-1812

IN THE MATTER OF	§	IN THE DISTRICT COURT
THE MARRIAGE OF	§	
	§	
JANE SMITH	§	
AND	§	1ST JUDICIAL DISTRICT
JOHN SMITH	§	
	§	
AND IN THE INTEREST OF	§	
JOAN SMITH, A CHILD	§	PURPLE COUNTY, TEXAS

EMPLOYER'S ORDER TO WITHHOLD FROM EARNINGS FOR CHILD SUPPORT

The Court ORDERS you, the employer of John Smith, Obligor, to withhold income from his disposable earnings from this employment as follows:

Obligor

Name: John Smith

Address: 801 Lonely Lane, Somewhere, Texas 77777

Social Security number: 888-88-8888

Obligee

Name: Jane Smith

Social Security number: 999-99-9999

Child

Name: Joan Smith

Sex: Female

Birth date:

Social Security number: 777-77-7777

Attached to this order is a copy of subchapter C, chapter 158, of the Texas Family Code, which sets forth rights, duties, and potential liabilities of employers in addition to the provisions of this order.

The Court ORDERS that any employer of John Smith shall begin withholding from his disposable earnings no later than the first pay period following the date this order is served on that employer.

The Court ORDERS the employer, on each pay date, to remit all amounts withheld through the Purple County Child Support Office, Purple County Courthouse, Somewhere, Texas 77777 for distribution according to law. The Court ORDERS the employer to include the following information with each payment: (1) the date of withholding; (2) the number assigned by the title IV-D agency (if available), the county identification number (if available), or the cause number, which is 01-1812; (3) John Smith's name; and (4) unless the payment is transmitted by electronic funds transfer, Jane Smith's name.

Maximum Amount Withheld

The maximum amount to be withheld shall not exceed 50 percent of John Smith's disposable earnings.

"Arrearage" Defined

As used in this order, the term "arrearage" means the sum of:

1. all past-due child-support and medical-support payments; and

2. all unpaid interest accrued on child-support and medical-support obligations; and

3. all unpaid child-support and medical-support judgment amounts.

The Court ORDERS the employer to withhold the following amounts from the earnings of John Smith:

$500.00   if Obligor is PAID MONTHLY:

                $500 on current support,

                $0.00 on the arrearage owed, and

                $0.00 on fees and costs.

$250.00   if Obligor is PAID TWICE MONTHLY:

                $250.00 on current support,

                $0.00 on the arrearage owed, and

                $0.00 on fees and costs.

$230.77   if Obligor is PAID EVERY OTHER WEEK:

                $230.77 on current support,

                $0.00 on the arrearage and

                $0.00 on fees and costs.

$115.39   if Obligor is PAID EVERY WEEK:

$115.39 on current support,

$0.00 on the arrearage and

$0.00 on fees and costs.

The Court ORDERS the employer to withhold the above amount until the first month following the date of the earliest occurrence of one of the events specified below:

1. the child reaches the age of eighteen years, provided that, if the child is fully enrolled in an accredited secondary school in a program leading toward a high school diploma or enrolled in courses for joint high school and junior college credit pursuant to Section 130.008, Education Code, the periodic child-support payments shall continue to be due and paid until the end of the month in which the child graduates from high school;

2. the child marries;

3. the child dies;

4. the child's disabilities are otherwise removed for general purposes; or

5. further order modifying this child support.

Calculating Disposable Earnings

The employer shall calculate John Smith's disposable earnings, which are subject to withholding for child support, as follows:

1. Determine the "earnings" of John Smith. "Earnings" means a payment to or due an individual, regardless of source and how denominated, and includes a periodic or lump-sum payment for wages, salary, compensation received as an independent contractor, overtime pay, severance pay, commission, bonus, and interest income; payments made under a pension, an annuity, workers' compensation, and a disability or retirement program; and unemployment benefits.

2. Subtract the following sums to calculate John Smith's "disposable earnings":

a. any amounts required by law to be withheld, that is, federal income tax and federal FICA or OASI tax (Social Security) and Railroad Retirement Act contributions;

b. union dues;

c. nondiscretionary retirement contributions by John Smith; and

d. medical, hospitalization, and disability insurance coverage for John Smith and his child.

If you receive more than one "Writ of Withholding" or "Employer's Order to Withhold Earnings for Child Support" for John Smith, you shall pay an equal amount towards the current support portion of all orders or writs until each is individually complied with, and thereafter pay equal amounts on the arrearage portion of all orders or writs until each is complied with, or until the maximum total amount of allowable withholding, 50 percent of John Smith's disposable earnings, is reached, whichever occurs first.

For as long as John Smith is employed by you, you, the employer of John Smith, shall continue to withhold income in accordance with this order until the youngest child reaches eighteen years of age or graduates from high school, whichever occurs last. This order indicates when the child reaches eighteen years of age. Written notice from the child's school of the child's high-school graduation will constitute notice of graduation to you.

The Court ORDERS the employer to notify the Court and Jane Smith within seven days of the date that John Smith terminates employment. The Court ORDERS the employer to provide John Smith's last known address and the name and address of his new employer, if known.

SIGNED on _____.

_____

JUDGE PRESIDING

NO. 01-1812

IN THE MATTER OF	§	IN THE DISTRICT COURT
THE MARRIAGE OF	§	
	§	
JANE SMITH	§	
AND	§	1ST JUDICIAL DISTRICT
JOHN SMITH	§	
	§	
AND IN THE INTEREST OF	§	
JOAN SMITH, A CHILD	§	PURPLE COUNTY, TEXAS

FINANCIAL INFORMATION STATEMENT
FOR HEARINGS ON TEMPORARY ORDERS

This statement is submitted by JANE SMITH, Wife.

1. Date of marriage: SEPTEMBER 9, 1985

2. Date of separation: JANUARY 1, 2001

3. Age of child of this marriage:
   JOAN SMITH   Age: 10 years

4. Wife's occupation: Accountant

5. Wife's gross earnings from
   primary employment per month $3000

   Withholding/FICA $150

   Insurance $75

   Retirement $75

   Other $0

              Total deductions $300.00

   Wife's net income from primary
   employment per month $2,700.00

   Wife's average income from

other sources per month $0

Wife's net income per month $2,700.00

(Please attach applicable 1040s, W-2s or most recent pay stub.)

6   Necessary monthly living expenses:

House payment or rent $800
(include second mortgage, insurance,
taxes, condominium assessments)

Utilities including telephone $175

Food including school lunches $300

Child care $250

Car payments and auto insurance $350

Gasoline, oil, parking, bus fares, tolls, repairs $150

Attorney's fees $0

Health and life insurance premiums $0
(exclude company-paid insurance)

Uninsured medical and drug expenses $25

Uninsured dental and orthodontic expenses $25

Uninsured mental health care expenses $0

Clothing and laundry $100

Personal (entertainment, adult education, etc.) $100

Minimum monthly debt service (see item 9. below) $100.00

                    Total $2,375.00

7.   Debts (exclude house mortgage and car payments):

Creditor	Balance of Debt	Minimum Monthly Payment
Visa	$4000	$100

8.   Funds and assets readily convertible into cash in control of Husband:

Accounts in financial institutions $100,000

(banks, savings and loans, credit unions,
certificates of deposit)

Stocks and bonds $150,000

9. Funds and assets readily convertible into cash in control of Wife:

Accounts in financial institutions $50,000

Stocks and bonds $50,000

SIGNED on _____.

_____
Wife

NO. 01-1812

IN THE MATTER OF	§	IN THE DISTRICT COURT
THE MARRIAGE OF	§	
	§	
JANE SMITH	§	
AND	§	1ST JUDICIAL DISTRICT
JOHN SMITH	§	
	§	
AND IN THE INTEREST OF	§	
JOAN SMITH, A CHILD	§	PURPLE COUNTY, TEXAS

NOTICE OF INTENTION TO TAKE ORAL DEPOSITION OF JOHN SMITH

To: JOHN SMITH, by and through his attorney of record, Legal B. Eagle.

Under rule 199 of the Texas Rules of Civil Procedure, you are notified that you are required to be present and give your oral deposition in this case at the offices of Legal B. Eagle, 6666 Barrister St., Somewhere, Texas 77777 on August 1, 2001 at10:00 a.m.. This deposition will be taken before an officer authorized by law to take depositions and will continue from day to day until completed. This deposition will not be taken by telephone or other remote electronic means. This deposition will be recorded by videotape. It will also be recorded by stenographic means.

You are further notified that you are required to bring with you to the above address on the above date all documents in your possession or within your access by law or in fact set forth in Exhibit A attached to this notice and incorporated in it by reference for all purposes and permit Petitioner to inspect and copy each of those documents.

Jane Smith
210 Happy Trails
Somewhere, Texas 77777
555-555-5555
Petitioner

Certificate of Service

I certify that a true copy of the above was served on each attorney of record or party in accordance with the Texas Rules of Civil Procedure on July 26, 2001.

_____

Jane Smith

Exhibit A

The terms "documents," "writings," and "records" are used in this exhibit in their customary broad sense and include without limitation the following items, regardless of origin or location, whether printed, recorded, filmed, or reproduced by any other mechanical process or written or produced by hand; whether or not claimed to be privileged against discovery on any ground; and whether an original, master, or copy.

You are to produce, if you have not previously produced, the following documents:

1. All income tax returns for the past 5 years

2. All documents reflecting money earned by John Smith in the past 12 months.

NO. 01-1812

IN THE MATTER OF	§	IN THE DISTRICT COURT
THE MARRIAGE OF	§	
	§	
JANE SMITH	§	1ST JUDICIAL DISTRICT
AND	§	
JOHN SMITH	§	
	§	
AND IN THE INTEREST OF	§	PURPLE COUNTY, TEXAS
JOAN SMITH, A CHILD	§	

MOTION FOR JUDGE TO CONFER WITH CHILD

This Motion to Confer is brought by Jane Smith, Petitioner, who would show the Court as follows:

1. The issue of managing conservatorship of the child is contested.

2. For the purpose of determining the best interest of the child, Jane Smith requests that the Court confer with the child in chambers to determine the child's wishes. Petitioner requests that the Court conduct this interview outside the presence of counsel.

3. Jane Smith requests that a record of the interview be made and included as a part of the record in this case.

Jane Smith prays that the Court grant this Motion to Confer.

Respectfully submitted,

_____

Jane Smith
210 Happy Trails
Somewhere, Texas 77777
555/555-1234

Certificate of Service

I certify that a true and correct copy of the above and foregoing was served on all parties in accordance with the Texas Rules of Civil Procedure on _____.

_____
Jane Smith

Notice of Hearing

The above motion is set for hearing on _____ at ___.m. in the 1st District Court, Purple County Courthouse, Purple, Texas.

SIGNED on _____.

_____
JUDGE PRESIDING

ORDER

On the ____ day of _____, 2001, came to be heard Petitioner's Motion to Confer. The Court, after considering the pleadings, evidence, and argument of counsel, finds that the Motion is granted. IT IS FURTHER ORDERED that counsel shall not be present for the interview.

SIGNED on _____.

_____
JUDGE PRESIDING

NO. 01-1812

IN THE MATTER OF	§	IN THE DISTRICT COURT
THE MARRIAGE OF	§	
	§	
JANE SMITH	§	1ST JUDICIAL DISTRICT
AND	§	
JOHN SMITH	§	
	§	
AND IN THE INTEREST OF	§	PURPLE COUNTY, TEXAS
JOAN SMITH, A CHILD	§	

CERTIFICATE OF LAST KNOWN MAILING ADDRESS

I hereby certify that the last known mailing address of John Smith, Respondent, is 801 Lonely Lane, Somewhere, Texas 77777.

Respectfully submitted,

_____

Jane Smith
210 Happy Trails
Somewhere, Texas 77777
555/555-1234

NO. 01-1812

IN THE MATTER OF	§	IN THE DISTRICT COURT
THE MARRIAGE OF	§	
	§	
JANE SMITH	§	
AND	§	1ST JUDICIAL DISTRICT
JOHN SMITH	§	
	§	
AND IN THE INTEREST OF	§	
JOAN SMITH, A CHILD	§	PURPLE COUNTY, TEXAS

TEMPORARY ORDERS

On May 15, 2001 the Court heard Petitioner's motion for temporary orders.

Petitioner, Jane Smith, appeared in person and announced ready.

Respondent, John Smith, appeared in person and announced ready.

The Court, after examining the record and the agreement of the parties and hearing the evidence and argument of counsel, finds that all necessary prerequisites of the law have been legally satisfied and that the Court has jurisdiction of this case and of all the parties.

The Court finds that the following orders for the safety and welfare of the child, Joan Smith, are in the best interest of the child.

IT IS ORDERED that Jane Smith and John Smith are appointed Temporary Joint Managing Conservators of the following child: Joan Smith.

IT IS ORDERED that, at all times, Jane Smith, as a parent temporary joint managing conservator, shall have the following rights and duty:

1.   the right to receive information from the other parent concerning the health, education, and welfare of the child;

2.   the duty to inform the other parent in a timely manner of significant information concerning the health, education, and welfare of the child;

3.   the right to confer with the other parent to the extent possible before making a decision concerning the health, education, and welfare of the child;

4.   the right of access to medical, dental, psychological, and educational records of the child;

5. the right to consult with a physician, dentist, or psychologist of the child;

6. the right to consult with school officials concerning the child's welfare and educational status, including school activities;

7. the right to attend school activities;

8. the right to be designated on the child's records as a person to be notified in case of an emergency;

9. the right to consent to medical, dental, and surgical treatment during an emergency involving an immediate danger to the health and safety of the child; and

10. the right to manage the estate of the child to the extent the estate has been created by the parent or the parent's family.

IT IS ORDERED that, at all times, John Smith, as a parent temporary joint managing conservator, shall have the following rights and duty:

1. the right to receive information from the other parent concerning the health, education, and welfare of the child;

2. the duty to inform the other parent in a timely manner of significant information concerning the health, education, and welfare of the child;

3. the right to confer with the other parent to the extent possible before making a decision concerning the health, education, and welfare of the child;

4. the right of access to medical, dental, psychological, and educational records of the child;

5. the right to consult with a physician, dentist, or psychologist of the child;

6. the right to consult with school officials concerning the child's welfare and educational status, including school activities;

7. the right to attend school activities;

8. the right to be designated on the child's records as a person to be notified in case of an emergency;

9. the right to consent to medical, dental, and surgical treatment during an emergency involving an immediate danger to the health and safety of the child; and

10. the right to manage the estate of the child to the extent the estate has been created by the parent or the parent's family.

IT IS ORDERED that, during her respective periods of possession, Jane Smith, as a parent temporary joint managing conservator, shall have the following rights and duties:

1.   the duty of care, control, protection, and reasonable discipline of the child;

2.   the duty to support the child, including providing the child with clothing, food, shelter, and medical and dental care not involving an invasive procedure;

3.   the right to consent for the child to medical and dental care not involving an invasive procedure;

4.   the right to consent for the child to medical, dental, and surgical treatment during an emergency involving immediate danger to the health and safety of the child; and

5.   the right to direct the moral and religious training of the child.

IT IS ORDERED that, during his respective periods of possession, John Smith, as a parent temporary joint managing conservator, shall have the following rights and duties:

1.   the duty of care, control, protection, and reasonable discipline of the child;

2.   the duty to support the child, including providing the child with clothing, food, shelter, and medical and dental care not involving an invasive procedure;

3.   the right to consent for the child to medical and dental care not involving an invasive procedure;

4.   the right to consent for the child to medical, dental, and surgical treatment during an emergency involving immediate danger to the health and safety of the child; and

5.   the right to direct the moral and religious training of the child.

IT IS ORDERED that Jane Smith, as a parent temporary joint managing conservator, shall have the following rights and duty:

1.   the right to establish the primary residence of the child;

2.   the right to consent to medical, dental, and surgical treatment involving invasive procedures and to consent to psychiatric and psychological treatment of the child;

3.   the right to receive and give receipt for periodic payments for the support of the child and to hold or disburse these funds for the benefit of the child;

4.   the right to represent the child in legal action and to make other decisions of substantial legal significance concerning the child;

5.   the right to consent to marriage and to enlistment in the armed forces of the United States;

6.   the right to make decisions concerning the child's education;

7.   the right to the services and earnings of the child;

8.   except when a guardian of the child's estate or a guardian or attorney ad litem has been appointed for the child, the right to act as an agent of the child in relation to the

child's estate if the child's action is required by a state, the United States, or a foreign government; and

9. the duty to manage the estate of the child to the extent the estate has been created by community property or the joint property of the parents.

IT IS ORDERED that Jane Smith shall have the exclusive right to establish the domicile of the child.

IT IS ORDERED that each parent shall have the duty to inform the other parent if the parent resides with for at least 30 days, marries, or intends to marry a person who the parent knows: 1) is registered as a sex offender under Chapter 62, Code of Criminal Procedure; or 2) is currently charged with an offense for which on conviction the person would be required to register under that chapter. This notice shall be made as soon as practicable but not later than the 40th day after the date the parent begins to reside with the person or the 10th day after the date the marriage occurs, as appropriate. The notice must include a description of the offense that is the basis of the person's requirement to register as a sex offender or of the offense with which the person is charged.

Standard Possession Order

The Court finds that the following provisions of this Standard Possession Order are intended to and do comply with the requirements of Texas Family Code sections 153.311 through 153.317. IT IS ORDERED that the conservators shall comply with all terms and conditions of this Standard Possession Order. IT IS ORDERED that this Standard Possession Order is effective immediately and applies to all periods of possession occurring on and after the signing of this Standard Possession Order. IT IS, THEREFORE, ORDERED:

(a) Definitions

1. In this Standard Possession Order "school" means the primary or secondary school in which the child is enrolled or, if the child is not enrolled in a primary or secondary school, the public school district in which the child primarily resides.

2. In this Standard Possession Order "child" includes each child, whether one or more, who is a subject of this suit while that child is under the age of eighteen years and not otherwise emancipated.

(b) Mutual Agreement or Specified Terms for Possession

IT IS ORDERED that the conservators shall have possession of the child at times mutually agreed to in advance by the parties, and, in the absence of mutual agreement, it is ORDERED that the conservators shall have possession of the child under the specified terms set out in this Standard Possession Order.

(c)   Parents Who Reside 100 Miles or Less Apart

Except as otherwise explicitly provided in this Standard Possession Order, when John Smith resides 100 miles or less from the primary residence of the child, John Smith shall have the right to possession of the child as follows:

1.   Weekends - On weekends, beginning at the time the child's school is regularly dismissed, on the first, third, and fifth Friday of each month and ending at the time the child's school resumes after the weekend.

2.   Weekend Possession Extended by a Holiday - Except as otherwise explicitly provided in this Standard Possession Order, if a weekend period of possession by John Smith begins on a Friday that is a school holiday during the regular school term or a federal, state, or local holiday during the summer months when school is not in session, or if the period ends on or is immediately followed by a Monday that is such a holiday, that weekend period of possession shall begin at the time the child's school is regularly dismissed on the Thursday immediately preceding the Friday holiday or school holiday or end at the time school resumes after that holiday, as applicable.

3.   Wednesdays - On Wednesday of each week during the regular school term, beginning at the time the child's school is regularly dismissed and ending at the time the child's school resumes on Thursday.

4.   Christmas Holidays in Even-Numbered Years - In even-numbered years, beginning at the time the child's school is regularly dismissed on the day the child is dismissed from school for the Christmas school vacation and ending at noon on December 26.

5.   Christmas Holidays in Odd-Numbered Years - In odd-numbered years, beginning at noon on December 26 and ending at the time the child's school resumes after that Christmas school vacation.

6.   Thanksgiving in Odd-Numbered Years - In odd-numbered years, beginning at the time the child's school is regularly dismissed on the day the child is dismissed from school for the Thanksgiving holiday and ending at the time the child's school resumes after that Thanksgiving holiday.

7.   Spring Break in Even-Numbered Years - In even-numbered years, beginning at the time the child's school is regularly dismissed on the day the child is dismissed from school for the school's spring vacation and ending at the time school resumes after that vacation.

8.   Extended Summer Possession by John Smith

With Written Notice by April 1 - If John Smith gives Jane Smith written notice by April 1 of a year specifying an extended period or periods of summer possession for that year,

John Smith shall have possession of the child for thirty days beginning no earlier than the day after the child's school is dismissed for the summer vacation and ending no later than seven days before school resumes at the end of the summer vacation in that year, to be exercised in no more than two separate periods of at least seven consecutive days each, as specified in the written notice. These periods of possession shall begin and end at 6:00 p.m.

Without Written Notice by April 1 - If John Smith does not give Jane Smith written notice by April 1 of a year specifying an extended period or periods of summer possession for that year, John Smith shall have possession of the child for thirty consecutive days in that year beginning at 6:00 p.m. on July 1 and ending at 6:00 p.m. on July 31.

9. Child's Birthday - If John Smith is not otherwise entitled under this Standard Possession Order to present possession of the child on the child's birthday, John Smith shall have possession of the child beginning at 6:00 p.m. and ending at 8:00 p.m. on that day, provided that John Smith picks up the child from Jane Smith's residence and returns the child to that same place.

10. Father's Day Weekend - Each year, beginning at 6:00 p.m. on the Friday preceding Father's Day and ending at 6:00 p.m. on Father's Day, provided that if he is not otherwise entitled under this Standard Possession Order to present possession of the child, he shall pick up the child from Jane Smith's residence and return the child to that same place.

Notwithstanding the weekend and Wednesday periods of possession ORDERED for John Smith, it is explicitly ORDERED that Jane Smith shall have a superior right of possession of the child as follows:

1. Christmas Holidays in Odd-Numbered Years - In odd-numbered years, beginning at 6:00 p.m. on the day the child is dismissed from school for the Christmas school vacation and ending at noon on December 26.

2. Christmas Holidays in Even-Numbered Years - In even-numbered years, beginning at noon on December 26 and ending at 6:00 p.m. on the day before school resumes after that Christmas school vacation.

3. Thanksgiving in Even-Numbered Years - In even-numbered years, beginning at 6:00 p.m. on the day the child is dismissed from school for the Thanksgiving holiday and ending at 6:00 p.m. on the following Sunday.

4. Spring Break in Odd-Numbered Years - In odd-numbered years, beginning at 6:00 p.m. on the day the child is dismissed from school for the school's spring vacation and ending at 6:00 p.m. on the day before school resumes after that vacation.

5. Summer Weekend Possession by Jane Smith - If Jane Smith gives John Smith written notice by April 15 of a year, Jane Smith shall have possession of the child on any one

weekend beginning at 6:00 p.m. on Friday and ending at 6:00 p.m. on the following Sunday during any one period of the extended summer possession by John Smith in that year, provided that Jane Smith picks up the child from John Smith and returns the child to that same place.

6.   Extended Summer Possession by Jane Smith - If Jane Smith gives John Smith written notice by April 15 of a year or gives John Smith fourteen days' written notice on or after April 16 of a year, Jane Smith may designate one weekend beginning no earlier than the day after the child's school is dismissed for the summer vacation and ending no later than seven days before school resumes at the end of the summer vacation, during which an otherwise scheduled weekend period of possession by John Smith shall not take place in that year, provided that the weekend so designated does not interfere with John Smith's period or periods of extended summer possession or with Father's Day Weekend.

7.   Child's Birthday - If Jane Smith is not otherwise entitled under this Standard Possession Order to present possession of the child on the child's birthday, Jane Smith shall have possession of the child beginning at 6:00 p.m. and ending at 8:00 p.m. on that day, provided that Jane Smith picks up the child from John Smith's residence and returns the child to that same place.

8.   Mother's Day Weekend - Each year, beginning at 6:00 p.m. on the Friday preceding Mother's Day and ending at 6:00 p.m. on Mother's Day, provided that if Jane Smith is not otherwise entitled under this Standard Possession Order to present possession of the child, she shall pick up the child from John Smith's residence and return the child to that same place.

Jane Smith shall have the right of possession of the child at all other times not specifically designated in this Standard Possession Order for John Smith.

(d)   Parents Who Reside More Than 100 Miles Apart

Except as otherwise explicitly provided in this Standard Possession Order, when John Smith resides more than 100 miles from the residence of the child, John Smith shall have the right to possession of the child as follows:

1.   Weekends - Unless John Smith elects the alternative period of weekend possession described in the next paragraph, John Smith shall have the right to possession of the child on weekends, beginning at the time the child's school is regularly dismissed on the first, third, and fifth Friday of each month and ending at the time the child's school resumes after the weekend. Except as otherwise explicitly provided in this Standard Possession Order, if such a weekend period of possession by John Smith begins on a Friday that is a school holiday during the regular school term or a federal, state, or local holiday during the summer months when school is not in session, or if the period ends on or is immediately followed by

a Monday that is such a holiday, that weekend period of possession shall begin at the time the child's school is regularly dismissed on the Thursday immediately preceding the Friday holiday or school holiday or end at the time school resumes after that holiday, as applicable.

Alternate weekend possession - In lieu of the weekend possession described in the foregoing paragraph, John Smith shall have the right to possession of the child not more than one weekend per month of John Smith's choice beginning at the time the child's school is regularly dismissed on the day school recesses for the weekend and ending at the time school resumes after the weekend. Except as otherwise explicitly provided in this Standard Possession Order, if such a weekend period of possession by John Smith begins on a Friday that is a school holiday during the regular school term or a federal, state, or local holiday during the summer months when school is not in session, or if the period ends on or is immediately followed by a Monday that is such a holiday, that weekend period of possession shall begin at the time the child's school is regularly dismissed on the Thursday immediately preceding the Friday holiday or school holiday or end at the time school resumes after that holiday, as applicable. John Smith may elect an option for this alternative period of weekend possession by giving written notice to Jane Smith within ninety days after the parties begin to reside more than 100 miles apart. If John Smith makes this election, John Smith shall give Jane Smith fourteen days' written or telephonic notice preceding a designated weekend. The weekends chosen shall not conflict with the provisions regarding Christmas, Thanksgiving, the child's birthday, and Mother's Day Weekend below.

2.   Christmas Holidays in Even-Numbered Years - In even-numbered years, beginning at the time the child's school is regularly dismissed on the day the child is dismissed from school for the Christmas school vacation and ending at noon on December 26.

3.   Christmas Holidays in Odd-Numbered Years - In odd-numbered years, beginning at noon on December 26 and ending at the time the child's school resumes after that Christmas school vacation.

4.   Thanksgiving in Odd-Numbered Years - In odd-numbered years, beginning at the time the child's school is regularly dismissed on the day the child is dismissed from school for the Thanksgiving holiday and ending at the time the child's school resumes after that Thanksgiving holiday.

5.   Spring Break in All Years - Every year, beginning at the time the child's school is regularly dismissed on the day the child is dismissed from school for the school's spring vacation and ending at the time school resumes after that vacation.

6.   Extended Summer Possession by John Smith -

With Written Notice by April 1 - If John Smith gives Jane Smith written notice by April 1 of a year specifying an extended period or periods of summer possession for that year,

John Smith shall have possession of the child for forty-two days beginning no earlier than the day after the child's school is dismissed for the summer vacation and ending no later than seven days before school resumes at the end of the summer vacation in that year, to be exercised in no more than two separate periods of at least seven consecutive days each, as specified in the written notice. These periods of possession shall begin and end at 6:00 p.m.

Without Written Notice by April 1 - If John Smith does not give Jane Smith written notice by April 1 of a year specifying an extended period or periods of summer possession for that year, John Smith shall have possession of the child for forty-two consecutive days beginning at 6:00 p.m. on June 15 and ending at 6:00 p.m. on July 27 of that year.

7.   Child's Birthday - If John Smith is not otherwise entitled under this Standard Possession Order to present possession of the child on the child's birthday, John Smith shall have possession of the child beginning at 6:00 p.m. and ending at 8:00 p.m. on that day, provided that John Smith picks up the child from Jane Smith's residence and returns the child to that same place.

8.   Father's Day Weekend - Each year, beginning at 6:00 p.m. on the Friday preceding Father's Day and ending at 6:00 p.m. on Father's Day, provided that if John Smith is not otherwise entitled under this Standard Possession Order to present possession of the child, he shall pick up the child from Jane Smith's residence and return the child to that same place.

Notwithstanding the weekend periods of possession ORDERED for John Smith, it is explicitly ORDERED that Jane Smith shall have a superior right of possession of the child as follows:

1.   Christmas Holidays in Odd-Numbered Years - In odd-numbered years, beginning at 6:00 p.m. on the day the child is dismissed from school for the Christmas school vacation and ending at noon on December 26.

2.   Christmas Holidays in Even-Numbered Years - In even-numbered years, beginning at noon on December 26 and ending at 6:00 p.m. on the day before school resumes after that Christmas school vacation.

3.   Thanksgiving in Even-Numbered Years - In even-numbered years, beginning at 6:00 p.m. on the day the child is dismissed from school for the Thanksgiving holiday and ending at 6:00 p.m. on the following Sunday.

4.   Summer Weekend Possession by Jane Smith - If Jane Smith gives John Smith written notice by April 15 of a year, Jane Smith shall have possession of the child on any one weekend beginning at 6:00 p.m. on Friday and ending at 6:00 p.m. on the following Sunday during any one period of possession by John Smith during John Smith's extended summer possession in that year, provided that if a period of possession by John Smith in that year

exceeds thirty days, Jane Smith may have possession of the child under the terms of this provision on any two nonconsecutive weekends during that period and provided that Jane Smith picks up the child from John Smith and returns the child to that same place.

5.   Extended Summer Possession by Jane Smith - If Jane Smith gives John Smith written notice by April 15 of a year, Jane Smith may designate twenty-one days beginning no earlier than the day after the child's school is dismissed for the summer vacation and ending no later than seven days before school resumes at the end of the summer vacation in that year, to be exercised in no more than two separate periods of at least seven consecutive days each, during which John Smith shall not have possession of the child, provided that the period or periods so designated do not interfere with John Smith's period or periods of extended summer possession or with Father's Day Weekend.

6.   Child's Birthday - If Jane Smith is not otherwise entitled under this Standard Possession Order to present possession of the child on the child's birthday, Jane Smith shall have possession of the child beginning at 6:00 p.m. and ending at 8:00 p.m. on that day, provided that Jane Smith picks up the child from John Smith's residence and returns the child to that same place.

7.   Mother's Day Weekend - Each year, beginning at 6:00 p.m. on the Friday preceding Mother's Day and ending at 6:00 p.m. on Mother's Day, provided that if Jane Smith is not otherwise entitled under this Standard Possession Order to present possession of the child, she shall pick up the child from John Smith's residence and return the child to that same place.

Jane Smith shall have the right of possession of the child at all other times not specifically designated in this Standard Possession Order for John Smith.

(e)   General Terms and Conditions

Except as otherwise explicitly provided in this Standard Possession Order, the terms and conditions of possession of the child that apply regardless of the distance between the residence of a parent and the child are as follows:

1.   Surrender of Child by Jane Smith - Jane Smith is ORDERED to surrender the child to John Smith at the beginning of each period of John Smith's possession at the residence of Jane Smith.

If a period of possession by John Smith begins at the time the child's school is regularly dismissed, Jane Smith is ORDERED to surrender the child to John Smith at the beginning of each such period of possession at the school in which the child is enrolled. If the child is not in school, John Smith shall pick up the child at the residence of Jane Smith at 210 Happy Trails, Somewhere, Texas, and Jane Smith is ORDERED to surrender the child to John Smith at the residence of Jane Smith at 210 Happy Trails, Somewhere, Texas under these circumstances.

2.   Return of Child by John Smith - John Smith is ORDERED to return the child to the residence of Jane Smith at the end of each period of possession. However, it is ORDERED that, if Jane Smith and John Smith live in the same county at the time of rendition of this order, John Smith's county of residence remains the same after rendition of this order, and Jane Smith's county of residence changes, effective on the date of the change of residence by Jane Smith, John Smith shall surrender the child to Jane Smith at the residence of John Smith at the end of each period of possession.

If a period of possession by John Smith ends at the time the child's school resumes, John Smith is ORDERED to surrender the child to Jane Smith at the end of each period of possession at the school in which the child is enrolled or, if the child is not in school, at the residence of Jane Smith at 210 Happy Trails, Somewhere, Texas.

3.   Surrender of Child by John Smith - John Smith is ORDERED to surrender the child to Jane Smith, if the child is in John Smith's possession or subject to John Smith's control, at the beginning of each period of Jane Smith's exclusive periods of possession, at the place designated in this Standard Possession Order.

4.   Return of Child by Jane Smith - Jane Smith is ORDERED to return the child to John Smith, if John Smith is entitled to possession of the child, at the end of each of Jane Smith's exclusive periods of possession, at the place designated in this Standard Possession Order.

5.   Personal Effects - Each conservator is ORDERED to return with the child the personal effects that the child brought at the beginning of the period of possession.

6.   Designation of Competent Adult - Each conservator may designate any competent adult to pick up and return the child, as applicable. IT IS ORDERED that a conservator or a designated competent adult be present when the child is picked up or returned.

7.   Inability to Exercise Possession - Each conservator is ORDERED to give notice to the person in possession of the child on each occasion that the conservator will be unable to exercise that conservator's right of possession for any specified period.

8.   Written Notice - Written notice shall be deemed to have been timely made if received or postmarked before or at the time that notice is due.

9.   Notice to School and Jane Smith - If John Smith's time of possession of the child ends at the time school resumes and for any reason the child is not or will not be returned to school, John Smith shall immediately notify the school and Jane Smith that the child will not be or has not been returned to school.

This concludes the Standard Possession Order.

Duration.

The periods of possession ordered above apply to the child the subject of this suit while that child is under the age of eighteen years and not otherwise emancipated.

Child Support.

IT IS ORDERED that John Smith is obligated to pay and shall pay to Jane Smith child support of $500 per month, with the first payment being due and payable on June 1, 2001 and a like payment being due and payable on the first day of each month thereafter until the first month following the date of the earliest occurrence of one of the events specified below:

1.   the child reaches the age of eighteen years, provided that, if the child is fully enrolled in an accredited secondary school in a program leading toward a high school diploma or enrolled in courses for joint high school and junior college credit pursuant to Section 130.008, Education Code, the periodic child-support payments shall continue to be due and paid until the end of the month in which the child graduates from high school;

2.   the child marries;

3.   the child dies;

4.   the child's disabilities are otherwise removed for general purposes; or

5.   further order modifying this child support.

Withholding from Earnings.

IT IS ORDERED that any employer of John Smith shall be ordered to withhold from earnings for child support from the disposable earnings of John Smith for the support of Joan Smith.

IT IS ORDERED that all payments shall be made through the Purple County Child Support Office, Purple County Courthouse, Somewhere, Texas 77777 and then remitted by that agency to Jane Smith for the support of the child. IT IS FURTHER ORDERED that John Smith shall pay, when due, all fees charged by that agency.

IT IS FURTHER ORDERED that John Smith shall notify this Court and Jane Smith by U.S. certified mail, return receipt requested, of any change of address and of any termination of employment. This notice shall be given no later than seven days after the change of address or the termination of employment. This notice or a subsequent notice shall also provide the current address of John Smith and the name and address of obligor's current employer, whenever that information becomes available.

IT IS ORDERED that, on the request of a prosecuting attorney, the attorney general, the friend of the Court, Jane Smith, or John Smith, the clerk of this Court shall cause a certified copy of the "Employer's Order to Withhold from Earnings for Child Support" to be delivered to any employer. IT IS FURTHER ORDERED that the clerk of this Court shall attach a copy of subchapter C of chapter 158 of the Texas Family Code for the information of any employer.

Health Care.

IT IS ORDERED that medical support shall be provided for the child as follows:

Respondent is ordered to obtain health insurance coverage for the child. The parties shall split all uninsured expenses equally.

No Credit for Informal Payments.

IT IS ORDERED that the child support as prescribed in this decree shall be exclusively discharged in the manner ordered and that any direct payments made by John Smith to Jane Smith or any expenditures incurred by John Smith during John Smith's periods of possession of or access to the child, as prescribed in this decree, for food, clothing, gifts, travel, shelter, or entertainment are deemed in addition to and not in lieu of the support ordered in this decree.

Support as Obligation of Estate.

IT IS ORDERED that the provisions for child support in this decree shall be an obligation of the estate of John Smith and shall not terminate on the death of John Smith. Payments received for the benefit of the child from the Social Security Administration, Department of Veterans Affairs, other government agency, or life insurance shall be a credit against this obligation.

Medical Notification.

Each party is ORDERED to inform the other party within twenty-four hours of any medical condition of the parties' child requiring surgical intervention, hospitalization, or both.

IT IS ORDERED that, at all times, Jane Smith, as a parent temporary joint managing conservator, shall have the following rights and duties:

IT IS ORDERED that each parent shall have the duty to inform the other parent if the parent resides with for at least 30 days, marries, or intends to marry a person who the parent knows: 1) is registered as a sex offender under Chapter 62, Code of Criminal Procedure; or 2) is currently charged with an offense for which on conviction the person would be required to register under that chapter. This notice shall be made as soon as practicable but not later than the 40th day after the date the parent begins to reside with the person or the 10th day after the date the marriage occurs, as appropriate. The notice must include a description of the offense that is the basis of the person's requirement to register as a sex offender or of the offense with which the person is charged.

IT IS ORDERED that Susan Social Worker prepare a social study into the circumstances and condition of the child and of the home of any person requesting managing conservatorship or possession of the child. The study shall be filed with the Court on or before July 1, 2001.

IT IS ORDERED that Dr. Abraham Lincoln is appointed to interview, examine, evaluate, and consult with the parties and the child to prepare a psychological evaluation of the parties and the child to be filed with the Court on or before July 1, 2001.

The Court finds that it is in the best interests of the child that the following temporary injunction be issued and related orders be entered.

IT IS ORDERED that the parties and their agents, servants, employees, attorneys, and those persons in active concert or participation with them who receive actual notice of this order by personal service or otherwise are temporarily enjoined from:

1.   Communicating with Petitioner in person, by telephone, or in writing in vulgar, profane, obscene, or indecent language or in a coarse or offensive manner.

2.   Threatening Petitioner in person, by telephone, or in writing to take unlawful action against any person.

3.   Placing one or more telephone calls, anonymously, at any unreasonable hour, in an offensive and repetitious manner, or without a legitimate purpose of communication.

4.   Causing bodily injury to Petitioner or to a child of either party.

5.   Threatening Petitioner or a child of either party with imminent bodily injury.

6.   Molesting or disturbing the peace of the child or of another party.

7.   Removing the child beyond the jurisdiction of the Court, acting directly or in concert with others.

8.   Disrupting or withdrawing the child from the school or day-care facility where the child is presently enrolled.

9.   Hiding or secreting the child from Petitioner or changing the child's current place of abode at 210 Happy Trails, Somewhere, Texas.

Information regarding each party is as follows:

Name: Jane Smith
Social Security number: 888-88-8888
Driver's license number and issuing state: Texas DL# 87654321
Current residence address: 210 Happy Trails, Somewhere, Texas 77777

Mailing address: 210 Happy Trails, Somewhere, Texas 77777

Home telephone number: 555-555-1234

Name of employer: Somewhere School District

Address of employment: 8 Learning Way, Somewhere, Texas

Work telephone number: 555/555-6666

Name: John Smith

Social Security number:

Driver's license number and issuing state: Texas DL# 12345678

Current residence address: 801 Lonely Lane, Somewhere, Texas 77777

Mailing address: 801 Lonely Lane, Somewhere, Texas 77777

Home telephone number: 555-555-5555

Name of employer: Big Company, Inc.

Address of employment: 1222 Corporate St., Somewhere, Texas 77777

Work telephone number: 555/555-3434

Name: Joan Smith

Social Security number: 777-77-7777

Driver's license number and issuing state: Texas DL# none

Current residence address: 210 Happy Trails, Somewhere, Texas 77777

Mailing address: 210 Happy Trails, Somewhere, Texas 77777

Home telephone number: 555-555-1234

Name of employer: none

Address of employment: none

Work telephone number: none

IT IS ORDERED that the parties must attend the Divorce Parent Education class.

These Temporary Orders shall continue in force until the signing of the Final Decree of Divorce or until further order of this Court.

SIGNED on _____.

_____

Judge Presiding

APPROVED AS TO BOTH FORM AND SUBSTANCE:

_____

_____

Typical Paternity Case—Case #2

The following hypothetical case is a story to apply to the forms that follow it. It is a fictitious scenario of a paternity action to demonstrate how petition, testing, and order forms would be completed based on such a case. The forms that follow are how this couple would use them. Should you decide to fill them in for yourself, you will have to retype them with your information.

Anna Rogers and Edward Hall were never married. Anna has had a child, Juana Rogers. She wants to get child support from the father, Edward Hall. Since they were not married, she has to file a paternity suit. Remember that Edward and Anna must also each submit the STATEMENT ON ALTERNATIVE DISPUTE RESOLUTION (form 21) with the first pleadings they file with the court. Edward initially denies that he is the father, so Anna requests DNA testing. This request is in her original petition. She sets a hearing, and serves a NOTICE OF HEARING on Edward using the NOTICE OF HEARING (form 20). When the judge orders the testing, Anna submits the ORDER FOR PARENTAL TESTING (form 16). If Edward decides not to request testing, he would sign the STATEMENT OF PATERNITY using form 17. Once the parties have either reached an agreement or had a trial, the FINAL ORDER IN SUIT TO ESTABLISH PARENTAGE, (form 18) will be completed.

TABLE OF FORMS FOR CASE #2

NO. 2212-99

IN THE INTEREST OF	§	IN THE DISTRICT COURT
	§	
JUANA ROGERS	§	001 JUDICIAL DISTRICT
	§	
A CHILD	§	URBAN COUNTY, TEXAS

ORDER FOR PARENTAGE TESTING

On _____ Respondent appeared by answer filed with the papers in this case. The Court finds that it is medically practical to take blood, body fluid, or tissue samples for parentage testing of the child who is the subject of this suit and that parentage testing is required by section 160.102 of the Texas Family Code.

IT IS THEREFORE ORDERED that the mother, ANNA ROGERS, and the alleged or probable father, EDWARD HALL, present themselves and that the child, JUANA ROGERS, be presented by the party who has physical possession of the child, each with appropriate photographic identification, at the following time, date, and location to submit to scientifically accepted parentage tests by the following qualified expert:

Name:	WHOSETHEDAD
Address:	222 Medical St., Urban, Texas 77777
Telephone:	555/555-5599
Time:	9:00 a..m.
Date:	January 1, 2002

All persons named above shall remain there until the parentage testing is complete and shall permit WHOSETHEDAD, or its designated agents or employees, to take blood, body fluid, or tissue samples sufficient for parentage testing. The expert shall perform testing sufficient to exclude at least 99 percent of the male population from the possibility of being the father and to ascertain the possibility or probability of the alleged father's parentage of the child, provided, however, that the expert shall not conduct any further testing without further order of the Court when that testing would bring the total cost of all testing under this order to an amount that exceeds $500.

SIGNED on _____.

_____
JUDGE PRESIDING

STATEMENT OF PATERNITY

State of Texas   §

County of Urban   §

Edward Hall, Affiant, appeared in person before me today and stated under oath:

"My name is Edward Hall. I am competent to make this affidavit. The facts stated in this affidavit are within my personal knowledge and are true and correct.

"I was born in Urban, Texas, on December 12, 1970 and am not now a minor. I now reside at 1212 Friendly, Urban, Texas 77777, Urban County, Texas. My Texas driver's license number is 12345678, and my Social Security number is 888-88-8888.

"I acknowledge that I am the biological father of the following child born to Anna Rogers:

Name: Juana Rogers

Sex: Female

Birthplace: Rural, Texas

Birth date: October 31, 2000"

_____
Edward Hall, Affiant

Verification

Edward Hall appeared in person before me today and stated on his oath that he is the Affiant, that he has read the foregoing Statement of Paternity, and that the statements in it are within his personal knowledge and are true and correct.

This Statement of Paternity was signed under oath before me on _____ by the Affiant.

_____
Notary Public

NO. 2212-99

IN THE INTEREST OF	§	IN THE DISTRICT COURT
	§	
JUANA ROGERS	§	001 JUDICIAL DISTRICT
	§	
A CHILD	§	URBAN COUNTY, TEXAS

PETITION TO ESTABLISH PARENTAGE

This suit is brought by ANNA ROGERS, who is 35 years of age and resides at 111 Singleton St., Urban, Texas 77777. Petitioner is the mother of the child the subject of this suit.

No court has continuing jurisdiction of this suit or of the child the subject of this suit.

The following child is the subject of this suit:

Name: JUANA ROGERS
Sex: Female
Birthplace: Rural, Texas
Birth date: October 31, 2000
Present residence: 111 Singleton St., Urban, Texas 77777

The alleged father of the child the subject of this suit is EDWARD HALL, whose age is 45 years and whose residence is 1212 Friendly, Urban, Texas 77777.

Process should be served at that address.

There are no court-ordered conservatorships, court-ordered guardianships, or other court-ordered relationships affecting the child the subject of this suit.

No property of consequence is owned or possessed by the child the subject of this suit.

The purpose of this suit is to establish the parent-child relationship between EDWARD HALL and the child the subject of this suit.

The best interest of the child the subject of this suit will be served by the appointment of ANNA ROGERS and EDWARD HALL as joint managing conservators, and Petitioner so requests. Petitioner further requests that appropriate orders be made for support of and access to the child. On a finding of parentage, Petitioner requests child support retroactive to the birth of the child and payment of an equitable portion of all prenatal and postnatal health-care expenses of the mother and the child.

Petitioner requests the name of the child JUANA ROGERS be ordered to be JUANA ROGERS HALL.

Petitioner requests the Court to appoint an investigator to prepare a social study into the circumstances and condition of the child and of the homes of all persons requesting conservatorship or possession of the child the subject of this suit.

Petitioner has signed a statement on alternative dispute resolution, which is attached as Exhibit 1.

Petitioner requests the Court, promptly after appearance of Respondent, to order the mother, the alleged or probable father, and the child to submit to parentage testing and to prescribe the arrangements for the tests.

Petitioner requests the Court to appoint one or more experts qualified in parentage testing to perform the tests and to order and provide for payment of any reasonable fees.

Petitioner requests that the arrangements prescribed by the Court for parentage testing include provisions for making blood, body fluid, or tissue samples available to WHOSETHEDAD, who is qualified in parentage testing and who is employed by Petitioner.

Petitioner requests that, after completion of the parentage testing, the Court order all parties to appear at a pretrial conference to hear the oral testimony or depositions concerning the tests and findings of the court-appointed experts and of any parentage-testing experts called by any party and, if appropriate, enter temporary orders under sections 105.011, 160.004, and 160.005 of the Texas Family Code.

Discovery will be conducted under level 2.

Petitioner prays that citation and notice issue as required by law.

Petitioner prays for judgment establishing parentage, that ANNA ROGERS be appointed managing conservator, that appropriate orders be made for the support of the child and for payment of an equitable portion of all prenatal and postnatal health-care expenses and of the fees, expenses, and costs of Petitioner in bringing this action, and that the child's name be ordered as requested above.

Petitioner prays for general relief.

Respectfully submitted,

_____

Anna Rogers
111 Singleton
Urban, Texas   77777
555-555-5567

NO. 2212-99

IN THE INTEREST OF	§	IN THE DISTRICT COURT
	§	
JUANA ROGERS	§	001 JUDICIAL DISTRICT
	§	
A CHILD	§	URBAN COUNTY, TEXAS

FINAL ORDER IN SUIT TO ESTABLISH PARENTAGE

On _____ the Court heard this case.

Petitioner, ANNA ROGERS, Social Security Number 111-11-1111 and Texas Driver's License Number 123456, appeared in person and through attorney of record, , and announced ready for trial.

Respondent, EDWARD HALL, Social Security number 222-22-2222, and 765432 Driver's License Number 765432, appeared in person and announced ready for trial.

The Court, after examining the record and hearing the evidence and argument of counsel, finds that it has jurisdiction of this case and of all the parties and that no other court has continuing, exclusive jurisdiction of this case. All questions of fact and of law were submitted to the Court. All persons entitled to citation were properly cited.

The record of testimony was duly reported by the court reporter for the 001 Judicial District Court.

The Court finds that the following child is the subject of this suit:

(a) Name: JUANA ROGERS

   Sex: Female

   Birthplace: Rural, Texas

   Birth date: October 31, 2000

   Present residence: 111 Singleton St., Urban, Texas 77777

   Home state: Texas

   Social Security number: 333-33-3333

   Driver's license number and issuing state: None

IT IS ORDERED that EDWARD HALL is, and he is declared to be, the father of the child JUANA ROGERS, born on October 31, 2000 to ANNA ROGERS, and that the parent-child relationship between the father and the child is established for all purposes.

The Court finds that the following orders are in the best interest of the child.

IT IS ORDERED that ANNA ROGERS and EDWARD HALL are appointed Joint Managing Conservators of the following child: JUANA ROGERS.

IT IS ORDERED that, at all times, ANNA ROGERS, as a parent joint managing conservator, shall have the following rights:

1.   the right to receive information from the other parent concerning the health, education, and welfare of the child;

2.   the right to confer with the other parent to the extent possible before making a decision concerning the health, education, and welfare of the child;

3.   the right of access to medical, dental, psychological, and educational records of the child;

4.   the right to consult with a physician, dentist, or psychologist of the child;

5.   the right to consult with school officials concerning the child's welfare and educational status, including school activities;

6.   the right to attend school activities;

7.   the right to be designated on the child's records as a person to be notified in case of an emergency;

8.   the right to consent to medical, dental, and surgical treatment during an emergency involving an immediate danger to the health and safety of the child; and

9.   the right to manage the estate of the child to the extent the estate has been created by the parent or the parent's family.

IT IS ORDERED that, at all times, ANNA ROGERS, as a parent joint managing conservator, shall have the following duties:

1.   the duty to inform the other parent in a timely manner of significant information concerning the health, education, and welfare of the child; and

2.   the duty to inform the other parent if the parent resides with for at least thirty days, marries, or intends to marry a person who the parent knows is registered as a sex offender under chapter 62 of the Code of Criminal Procedure (as added by chapter 668, Acts of the 75th Legislature, Regular Session, 1997) or is currently charged with an offense for which on conviction the person would be required to register under that chapter. IT IS ORDERED that this information shall be tendered in the form of a notice made as soon as practicable, but not later than the fortieth day after the date the parent begins to reside with

the person or on the tenth day after the date the marriage occurs, as appropriate. IT IS ORDERED that the notice must include a description of the offense that is the basis of the person's requirement to register as a sex offender or of the offense with which the person is charged. WARNING: A PERSON COMMITS AN OFFENSE PUNISHABLE AS A CLASS C MISDEMEANOR IF THE PERSON FAILS TO PROVIDE THIS NOTICE.

IT IS ORDERED that, at all times, EDWARD HALL, as a parent joint managing conservator, shall have the following rights:

1.   the right to receive information from the other parent concerning the health, education, and welfare of the child;

2.   the right to confer with the other parent to the extent possible before making a decision concerning the health, education, and welfare of the child;

3.   the right of access to medical, dental, psychological, and educational records of the child;

4.   the right to consult with a physician, dentist, or psychologist of the child;

5.   the right to consult with school officials concerning the child's welfare and educational status, including school activities;

6.   the right to attend school activities;

7.   the right to be designated on the child's records as a person to be notified in case of an emergency;

8.   the right to consent to medical, dental, and surgical treatment during an emergency involving an immediate danger to the health and safety of the child; and

9.   the right to manage the estate of the child to the extent the estate has been created by the parent or the parent's family.

IT IS ORDERED that, at all times, EDWARD HALL, as a parent joint managing conservator, shall have the following duties:

1.   the duty to inform the other parent in a timely manner of significant information concerning the health, education, and welfare of the child; and

2.   the duty to inform the other parent if the parent resides with for at least thirty days, marries, or intends to marry a person who the parent knows is registered as a sex offender under chapter 62 of the Code of Criminal Procedure (as added by chapter 668, Acts of the 75th Legislature, Regular Session, 1997) or is currently charged with an offense for which on conviction the person would be required to register under that chapter. IT IS ORDERED that this information shall be tendered in the form of a notice made as soon as practicable, but not later than the fortieth day after the date the parent begins to reside with

the person or on the tenth day after the date the marriage occurs, as appropriate. IT IS ORDERED that the notice must include a description of the offense that is the basis of the person's requirement to register as a sex offender or of the offense with which the person is charged. WARNING: A PERSON COMMITS AN OFFENSE PUNISHABLE AS A CLASS C MISDEMEANOR IF THE PERSON FAILS TO PROVIDE THIS NOTICE.

IT IS ORDERED that, during her respective periods of possession, ANNA ROGERS, as a parent joint managing conservator, shall have the following rights and duties:

1. the duty of care, control, protection, and reasonable discipline of the child;

2. the duty to support the child, including providing the child with clothing, food, shelter, and medical and dental care not involving an invasive procedure;

3. the right to consent for the child to medical and dental care not involving an invasive procedure;

4. the right to consent for the child to medical, dental, and surgical treatment during an emergency involving immediate danger to the health and safety of the child; and

5. the right to direct the moral and religious training of the child.

IT IS ORDERED that, during his respective periods of possession, EDWARD HALL, as a parent joint managing conservator, shall have the following rights and duties:

1. the duty of care, control, protection, and reasonable discipline of the child;

2. the duty to support the child, including providing the child with clothing, food, shelter, and medical and dental care not involving an invasive procedure;

3. the right to consent for the child to medical and dental care not involving an invasive procedure;

4. the right to consent for the child to medical, dental, and surgical treatment during an emergency involving immediate danger to the health and safety of the child; and

5. the right to direct the moral and religious training of the child.

IT IS ORDERED that ANNA ROGERS, as a parent joint managing conservator, shall have the following rights and duty:

1. the exclusive right to establish the primary residence of the child without regard to geographic location;

2. the right to consent to medical, dental, and surgical treatment involving invasive procedures and to consent to psychiatric and psychological treatment of the child;

3. the right to receive and give receipt for periodic payments for the support of the child and to hold or disburse these funds for the benefit of the child;

4. the right to represent the child in legal action and to make other decisions of substantial legal significance concerning the child;

5. the right to consent to marriage and to enlistment in the armed forces of the United States;

6. the right to make decisions concerning the child's education;

7. the right to the services and earnings of the child;

8. except when a guardian of the child's estate or a guardian or attorney ad litem has been appointed for the child, the independent right to act as an agent of the child in relation to the child's estate if the child's action is required by a state, the United States, or a foreign government; and

9. the duty to manage the estate of the child to the extent the estate has been created by community property or the joint property of the parents.

IT IS ORDERED that EDWARD HALL, as a parent joint managing conservator, shall have the following rights and duty:

1. the right to consent to medical, dental, and surgical treatment involving invasive procedures and to consent to psychiatric and psychological treatment of the child;

2. the right to represent the child in legal action and to make other decisions of substantial legal significance concerning the child;

3. the right to consent to marriage and to enlistment in the armed forces of the United States;

4. the right to make decisions concerning the child's education;

5. the right to the services and earnings of the child;

6. except when a guardian of the child's estate or a guardian or attorney ad litem has been appointed for the child, the independent right to act as an agent of the child in relation to the child's estate if the child's action is required by a state, the United States, or a foreign government; and

7. the duty to manage the estate of the child to the extent the estate has been created by community property or the joint property of the parents.

IT IS ORDERED that ANNA ROGERS shall have the exclusive right to establish the child's primary residence without regard to geographical location.

Standard Possession Order

The Court finds that the following provisions of this Standard Possession Order are intended to and do comply with the requirements of Texas Family Code sections 153.311 through 153.317. IT IS ORDERED that the conservators shall comply with all terms and conditions of this Standard Possession Order. IT IS ORDERED that this Standard Possession Order is effective immediately and applies to all periods of possession occurring on and after the signing of this Standard Possession Order. IT IS, THEREFORE, ORDERED:

(a)   Definitions

1.   In this Standard Possession Order "school" means the primary or secondary school in which the child is enrolled or, if the child is not enrolled in a primary or secondary school, the public school district in which the child primarily resides.

2.   In this Standard Possession Order "child" includes each child, whether one or more, who is a subject of this suit while that child is under the age of eighteen years and not otherwise emancipated.

(b)   Mutual Agreement or Specified Terms for Possession

IT IS ORDERED that the conservators shall have possession of the child at times mutually agreed to in advance by the parties, and, in the absence of mutual agreement, it is ORDERED that the conservators shall have possession of the child under the specified terms set out in this Standard Possession Order.

(c)   Parents Who Reside 100 Miles or Less Apart

Except as otherwise explicitly provided in this Standard Possession Order, when EDWARD HALL resides 100 miles or less from the primary residence of the child, EDWARD HALL shall have the right to possession of the child as follows:

1.   Weekends - On weekends, beginning at the time the child's school is regularly dismissed, on the first, third, and fifth Friday of each month and ending at the time the child's school resumes after the weekend.

2.   Weekend Possession Extended by a Holiday - Except as otherwise explicitly provided in this Standard Possession Order, if a weekend period of possession by EDWARD HALL begins on a Friday that is a school holiday during the regular school term or a federal, state, or local holiday during the summer months when school is not in session, or if the period ends on or is immediately followed by a Monday that is such a holiday, that weekend period of possession shall begin at the time the child's school is regularly dismissed on the Thursday immediately preceding the Friday holiday or school holiday or end at the time school resumes after that holiday, as applicable.

3. <u>Wednesdays</u> - On Wednesday of each week during the regular school term, beginning at the time the child's school is regularly dismissed and ending at the time the child's school resumes on Thursday..

4. <u>Christmas Holidays in Even-Numbered Years</u> - In even-numbered years, beginning at the time the child's school is regularly dismissed on the day the child is dismissed from school for the Christmas school vacation and ending at noon on December 26.

5. <u>Christmas Holidays in Odd-Numbered Years</u> - In odd-numbered years, beginning at noon on December 26 and ending at the time the child's school resumes after that Christmas school vacation.

6. <u>Thanksgiving in Odd-Numbered Years</u> - In odd-numbered years, beginning at the time the child's school is regularly dismissed on the day the child is dismissed from school for the Thanksgiving holiday and ending at the time the child's school resumes after that Thanksgiving holiday.

7. <u>Spring Break in Even-Numbered Years</u> - In even-numbered years, beginning at the time the child's school is regularly dismissed on the day the child is dismissed from school for the school's spring vacation and ending at the time school resumes after that vacation.

8. <u>Extended Summer Possession by EDWARD HALL</u>

<u>With Written Notice by April 1</u> - If EDWARD HALL gives ANNA ROGERS written notice by April 1 of a year specifying an extended period or periods of summer possession for that year, EDWARD HALL shall have possession of the child for thirty days beginning no earlier than the day after the child's school is dismissed for the summer vacation and ending no later than seven days before school resumes at the end of the summer vacation in that year, to be exercised in no more than two separate periods of at least seven consecutive days each, as specified in the written notice. These periods of possession shall begin and end at 6:00 p.m.

<u>Without Written Notice by April 1</u> - If EDWARD HALL does not give ANNA ROGERS written notice by April 1 of a year specifying an extended period or periods of summer possession for that year, EDWARD HALL shall have possession of the child for thirty consecutive days in that year beginning at 6:00 p.m. on July 1 and ending at 6:00 p.m. on July 31.

9. <u>Child's Birthday</u> - If EDWARD HALL is not otherwise entitled under this Standard Possession Order to present possession of the child on the child's birthday, EDWARD HALL shall have possession of the child beginning at 6:00 p.m. and ending at 8:00 p.m. on that day, provided that EDWARD HALL picks up the child from ANNA ROGERS's residence and returns the child to that same place.

10.   Father's Day Weekend - Each year, beginning at 6:00 p.m. on the Friday preceding Father's Day and ending at 6:00 p.m. on Father's Day, provided that if he is not otherwise entitled under this Standard Possession Order to present possession of the child, he shall pick up the child from ANNA ROGERS's residence and return the child to that same place.

Notwithstanding the weekend and Wednesday periods of possession ORDERED for EDWARD HALL, it is explicitly ORDERED that ANNA ROGERS shall have a superior right of possession of the child as follows:

1.   Christmas Holidays in Odd-Numbered Years - In odd-numbered years, beginning at 6:00 p.m. on the day the child is dismissed from school for the Christmas school vacation and ending at noon on December 26.

2.   Christmas Holidays in Even-Numbered Years - In even-numbered years, beginning at noon on December 26 and ending at 6:00 p.m. on the day before school resumes after that Christmas school vacation.

3.   Thanksgiving in Even-Numbered Years - In even-numbered years, beginning at 6:00 p.m. on the day the child is dismissed from school for the Thanksgiving holiday and ending at 6:00 p.m. on the following Sunday.

4.   Spring Break in Odd-Numbered Years - In odd-numbered years, beginning at 6:00 p.m. on the day the child is dismissed from school for the school's spring vacation and ending at 6:00 p.m. on the day before school resumes after that vacation.

5.   Summer Weekend Possession by ANNA ROGERS - If ANNA ROGERS gives EDWARD HALL written notice by April 15 of a year, ANNA ROGERS shall have possession of the child on any one weekend beginning at 6:00 p.m. on Friday and ending at 6:00 p.m. on the following Sunday during any one period of the extended summer possession by EDWARD HALL in that year, provided that ANNA ROGERS picks up the child from EDWARD HALL and returns the child to that same place.

6.   Extended Summer Possession by ANNA ROGERS - If ANNA ROGERS gives EDWARD HALL written notice by April 15 of a year or gives EDWARD HALL fourteen days' written notice on or after April 16 of a year, ANNA ROGERS may designate one weekend beginning no earlier than the day after the child's school is dismissed for the summer vacation and ending no later than seven days before school resumes at the end of the summer vacation, during which an otherwise scheduled weekend period of possession by EDWARD HALL shall not take place in that year, provided that the weekend so designated does not interfere with EDWARD HALL's period or periods of extended summer possession or with Father's Day Weekend.

7.   Child's Birthday - If ANNA ROGERS is not otherwise entitled under this Standard Possession Order to present possession of the child on the child's birthday, ANNA ROGERS shall have possession of the child beginning at 6:00 p.m. and ending at 8:00 p.m. on that day, provided that ANNA ROGERS picks up the child from EDWARD HALL's residence and returns the child to that same place.

8.   Mother's Day Weekend - Each year, beginning at 6:00 p.m. on the Friday preceding Mother's Day and ending at 6:00 p.m. on Mother's Day, provided that if ANNA ROGERS is not otherwise entitled under this Standard Possession Order to present possession of the child, she shall pick up the child from EDWARD HALL's residence and return the child to that same place.

ANNA ROGERS shall have the right of possession of the child at all other times not specifically designated in this Standard Possession Order for EDWARD HALL.

(d)   Parents Who Reside More Than 100 Miles Apart

Except as otherwise explicitly provided in this Standard Possession Order, when EDWARD HALL resides more than 100 miles from the residence of the child, EDWARD HALL shall have the right to possession of the child as follows:

1.   Weekends - Unless EDWARD HALL elects the alternative period of weekend possession described in the next paragraph, EDWARD HALL shall have the right to possession of the child on weekends, beginning at the time the child's school is regularly dismissed on the first, third, and fifth Friday of each month and ending at the time the child's school resumes after the weekend. Except as otherwise explicitly provided in this Standard Possession Order, if such a weekend period of possession by EDWARD HALL begins on a Friday that is a school holiday during the regular school term or a federal, state, or local holiday during the summer months when school is not in session, or if the period ends on or is immediately followed by a Monday that is such a holiday, that weekend period of possession shall begin at the time the child's school is regularly dismissed on the Thursday immediately preceding the Friday holiday or school holiday or end at the time school resumes after that holiday, as applicable.

Alternate weekend possession - In lieu of the weekend possession described in the foregoing paragraph, EDWARD HALL shall have the right to possession of the child not more than one weekend per month of EDWARD HALL's choice beginning at the time the child's school is regularly dismissed on the day school recesses for the weekend and ending at the time school resumes after the weekend. Except as otherwise explicitly provided in this Standard Possession Order, if such a weekend period of possession by EDWARD HALL begins on a Friday that is a school holiday during the regular school term or a federal, state, or local holiday during the summer months when school is not in session, or if the period ends on or is immediately followed by a Monday that is such a holiday, that weekend period of possession shall begin at the time the child's school is regularly dismissed on the Thursday immediately preceding the Friday holiday or school holiday or end at the time school resumes after that holiday, as applicable. EDWARD HALL may elect an option for this alternative period of weekend possession by giving written notice to ANNA ROGERS within ninety days after the parties begin to reside more than 100 miles apart. If EDWARD HALL makes this election, EDWARD HALL shall give ANNA ROGERS fourteen days' written or telephonic notice preceding a designated weekend. The weekends chosen shall not conflict with the provisions regarding Christmas, Thanksgiving, the child's birthday, and Father's Day Weekend below.

2.   <u>Christmas Holidays in Even-Numbered Years</u> - In even-numbered years, beginning at the time the child's school is regularly dismissed on the day the child is dismissed from school for the Christmas school vacation and ending at noon on December 26.

3.   <u>Christmas Holidays in Odd-Numbered Years</u> - In odd-numbered years, beginning at noon on December 26 and ending at the time the child's school resumes after that Christmas school vacation.

4.   <u>Thanksgiving in Odd-Numbered Years</u> - In odd-numbered years, beginning at the time the child's school is regularly dismissed on the day the child is dismissed from school for the Thanksgiving holiday and ending at the time the child's school resumes after that Thanksgiving holiday.

5.   <u>Spring Break in All Years</u> - Every year, beginning at the time the child's school is regularly dismissed on the day the child is dismissed from school for the school's spring vacation and ending at the time school resumes after that vacation.

6.   <u>Extended Summer Possession by EDWARD HALL</u> -

<u>With Written Notice by April 1</u> - If EDWARD HALL gives ANNA ROGERS written notice by April 1 of a year specifying an extended period or periods of summer possession for that year, EDWARD HALL shall have possession of the child for forty-two days beginning no earlier than the day after the child's school is dismissed for the summer vacation and ending no later than seven days before school resumes at the end of the summer vacation in that year, to be exercised in no more than two separate periods of at least seven consecutive days each, as specified in the written notice. These periods of possession shall begin and end at 6:00 p.m.

<u>Without Written Notice by April 1</u> - If EDWARD HALL does not give ANNA ROGERS written notice by April 1 of a year specifying an extended period or periods of summer possession for that year, EDWARD HALL shall have possession of the child for forty-two consecutive days beginning at 6:00 p.m. on June 15 and ending at 6:00 p.m. on July 27 of that year.

7.   <u>Child's Birthday</u> - If EDWARD HALL is not otherwise entitled under this

Standard Possession Order to present possession of the child on the child's birthday, EDWARD HALL shall have possession of the child beginning at 6:00 p.m. and ending at 8:00 p.m. on that day, provided that EDWARD HALL picks up the child from ANNA ROGERS's residence and returns the child to that same place.

8. <u>Father's Day Weekend</u> - Each year, beginning at 6:00 p.m. on the Friday preceding Father's Day and ending at 6:00 p.m. on Father's Day, provided that if EDWARD HALL is not otherwise entitled under this Standard Possession Order to present possession of the child, he shall pick up the child from ANNA ROGERS's residence and return the child to that same place.

Notwithstanding the weekend periods of possession ORDERED for EDWARD HALL, it is explicitly ORDERED that ANNA ROGERS shall have a superior right of possession of the child as follows:

1. <u>Christmas Holidays in Odd-Numbered Years</u> - In odd-numbered years, beginning at 6:00 p.m. on the day the child is dismissed from school for the Christmas school vacation and ending at noon on December 26.

2. <u>Christmas Holidays in Even-Numbered Years</u> - In even-numbered years, beginning at noon on December 26 and ending at 6:00 p.m. on the day before school resumes after that Christmas school vacation.

3. <u>Thanksgiving in Even-Numbered Years</u> - In even-numbered years, beginning at 6:00 p.m. on the day the child is dismissed from school for the Thanksgiving holiday and ending at 6:00 p.m. on the following Sunday.

4. <u>Summer Weekend Possession by ANNA ROGERS</u> - If ANNA ROGERS gives EDWARD HALL written notice by April 15 of a year, ANNA ROGERS shall have possession of the child on any one weekend beginning at 6:00 p.m. on Friday and ending at 6:00 p.m. on the following Sunday during any one period of possession by EDWARD HALL during EDWARD HALL's extended summer possession in that year, provided that if a period of possession by EDWARD HALL in that year exceeds thirty days, ANNA ROGERS may have possession of the child under the terms of this provision on any two nonconsecutive weekends during that period and provided that ANNA ROGERS picks up the child from EDWARD HALL and returns the child to that same place.

5. <u>Extended Summer Possession by ANNA ROGERS</u> - If ANNA ROGERS gives EDWARD HALL written notice by April 15 of a year, ANNA ROGERS may designate twenty-one days beginning no earlier than the day after the child's school is dismissed for the summer vacation and ending no later than seven days before school resumes at the end of the summer vacation in that year, to be exercised in no more than two separate periods of at least seven consecutive days each, during which EDWARD HALL shall not have possession of the

child, provided that the period or periods so designated do not interfere with EDWARD HALL's period or periods of extended summer possession or with Father's Day Weekend.

6.   Child's Birthday - If ANNA ROGERS is not otherwise entitled under this Standard Possession Order to present possession of the child on the child's birthday, ANNA ROGERS shall have possession of the child beginning at 6:00 p.m. and ending at 8:00 p.m. on that day, provided that ANNA ROGERS picks up the child from EDWARD HALL's residence and returns the child to that same place.

7.   Mother's Day Weekend - Each year, beginning at 6:00 p.m. on the Friday preceding Mother's Day and ending at 6:00 p.m. on Mother's Day, provided that if ANNA ROGERS is not otherwise entitled under this Standard Possession Order to present possession of the child, she shall pick up the child from EDWARD HALL's residence and return the child to that same place.

ANNA ROGERS shall have the right of possession of the child at all other times not specifically designated in this Standard Possession Order for EDWARD HALL.

(e)   General Terms and Conditions

Except as otherwise explicitly provided in this Standard Possession Order, the terms and conditions of possession of the child that apply regardless of the distance between the residence of a parent and the child are as follows:

1.   Surrender of Child by ANNA ROGERS - ANNA ROGERS is ORDERED to surrender the child to EDWARD HALL at the beginning of each period of EDWARD HALL's possession at the residence of ANNA ROGERS.

If a period of possession by EDWARD HALL begins at the time the child's school is regularly dismissed, ANNA ROGERS is ORDERED to surrender the child to EDWARD HALL at the beginning of each such period of possession at the school in which the child is enrolled. If the child is not in school, EDWARD HALL shall pick up the child at the residence of ANNA ROGERS and ANNA ROGERS is ORDERED to surrender the child to EDWARD HALL at the residence of ANNA ROGERS under these circumstances.

2.   Return of Child by EDWARD HALL - EDWARD HALL is ORDERED to return the child to the residence of ANNA ROGERS at the end of each period of possession. However, it is ORDERED that, if ANNA ROGERS and EDWARD HALL live in the same county at the time of rendition of this order, EDWARD HALL's county of residence remains the same after rendition of this order and ANNA ROGERS's county of residence changes, effective on the date of the change of residence by ANNA ROGERS, EDWARD HALL shall surrender the child to ANNA ROGERS at the residence of EDWARD HALL at the end of each period of possession.

If a period of possession by EDWARD HALL ends at the time the child's school resumes, EDWARD HALL is ORDERED to surrender the child to ANNA ROGERS at the end of each period of possession at the school in which the child is enrolled or, if the child is not in school, at the residence of ANNA ROGERS at .

3.   Surrender of Child by EDWARD HALL - EDWARD HALL is ORDERED to surrender the child to ANNA ROGERS, if the child is in EDWARD HALL's possession or subject to EDWARD HALL's control, at the beginning of each period of ANNA ROGERS's exclusive periods of possession, at the place designated in this Standard Possession Order.

4.   Return of Child by ANNA ROGERS - ANNA ROGERS is ORDERED to return the child to EDWARD HALL, if EDWARD HALL is entitled to possession of the child, at the end of each of ANNA ROGERS's exclusive periods of possession, at the place designated in this Standard Possession Order.

5.   Personal Effects - Each conservator is ORDERED to return with the child the personal effects that the child brought at the beginning of the period of possession.

6.   Designation of Competent Adult - Each conservator may designate any competent adult to pick up and return the child, as applicable. IT IS ORDERED that a conservator or a designated competent adult be present when the child is picked up or returned.

7.   Inability to Exercise Possession - Each conservator is ORDERED to give notice to the person in possession of the child on each occasion that the conservator will be unable to exercise that conservator's right of possession for any specified period.

8.   Written Notice - Written notice shall be deemed to have been timely made if received or postmarked before or at the time that notice is due.

9.   Notice to School and ANNA ROGERS - If EDWARD HALL's time of possession of the child ends at the time school resumes and for any reason the child is not or will not be returned to school, EDWARD HALL shall immediately notify the school and ANNA ROGERS that the child will not be or has not been returned to school.

This concludes the Standard Possession Order.

Duration.

The periods of possession ordered above apply to the child the subject of this suit while that child is under the age of eighteen years and not otherwise emancipated.

Termination of Orders on Marriage.

The provisions of this order relating to conservatorship, possession, or access terminate on the marriage of ANNA ROGERS to EDWARD HALL unless a nonparent or agency has been appointed conservator of the child under chapter 153 of the Texas Family Code.

IT IS ORDERED that EDWARD HALL is obligated to pay and shall pay to ANNA ROGERS child support of $750 per month, with the first payment being due and payable on January 1, 2002 and a like payment being due and payable on the first day of each month thereafter until the first month following the date of the earliest occurrence of one of the events specified below:

1.   the child reaches the age of eighteen years, provided that, if the child is fully enrolled in an accredited secondary school in a program leading toward a high school diploma or enrolled in courses for joint high school and junior college credit pursuant to Section 130.008 of the Texas Education Code, the periodic child-support payments shall continue to be due and paid until the end of the month in which the child graduates from high school;

2.   the child marries;

3.   the child dies;

4.   the child's disabilities are otherwise removed for general purposes;

5.   EDWARD HALL and ANNA ROGERS marry each other; or

6.   further order modifying this child support.

Withholding from Earnings.

IT IS ORDERED that any employer of EDWARD HALL shall be ordered to with-hold from earnings for child support from the disposable earnings of EDWARD HALL for the support of the child.

IT IS ORDERED that all payments shall be made through the Urban County Child Support Office, Urban County Courthouse, Urban, Texas 77777 and then remitted by that agency to ANNA ROGERS for the support of the child. IT IS FURTHER ORDERED that EDWARD HALL pay all fees charged by that agency.

IT IS FURTHER ORDERED that EDWARD HALL shall notify this Court and ANNA ROGERS by U.S. certified mail, return receipt requested, of any change of address and of any termination of employment. This notice shall be given no later than seven days after the change of address or the termination of employment. This notice or a subsequent notice shall also provide the current address of EDWARD HALL and the name and address of obligor's current employer, whenever that information becomes available.

IT IS ORDERED that, on the request of a prosecuting attorney, the attorney general, ANNA ROGERS, or EDWARD HALL, the clerk of this Court shall cause a certified copy of the "Order/Notice to Withhold Income for Child Support" to be delivered to any employer. IT IS FURTHER ORDERED that the clerk of this Court shall attach a copy of subchapter C of chapter 158 of the Texas Family Code for the information of any employer.

IT IS ORDERED that medical support shall be provided for the child as follows:

IT IS ORDERED that, as additional child support, Edward Hall shall provide health insurance for the parties' child, for as long as child support is payable under the terms of this decree, as set out herein.

"Health insurance" means insurance coverage that provides basic health-care services, including usual physician services, office visits, hospitalization, and laboratory, X-ray, and emergency services, and may be provided in the form of an indemnity insurance contract or plan, a preferred provider organization or plan, a health maintenance organization, or any combination thereof.

IT IS ORDERED that Edward Hall shall at his sole cost and expense, keep and maintain at all times in full force and effect the health insurance coverage that insures the parties' child through Edward Hall's employer, union, trade association, or other organization for as long as it is offered by his employer, union, trade association, or other organization. If his employer, union, trade association, or other organization subsequently changes health insurance benefits or carriers, Edward Hall is ORDERED to obtain and maintain coverage for the benefit of the child on the successor company or through such health insurance plan as is available through other employment, union, trade association, or other organization or other insurance provider.

IT IS ORDERED that if Edward Hall is leaving that employment, union, trade association, or other organization or for any other reason health insurance will not be available for the child through the employment or membership in a union, trade association, or other organization of either party, Edward Hall shall within ten days of termination of his or her employment or coverage, convert the policy to individual coverage for the child in an amount equal to or exceeding the coverage at the time his or her employment or coverage is terminated. Alternatively, if that health insurance was available through Anna Roger's employment or membership in a union, trade association, or other organization, Edward Hall shall reimburse Anna Rogers for the cost of the converted policy as follows: Edward Hall is ORDERED to pay to Anna Rogers at her last known address the cost of insuring the child under the converted policy, on the first day of each month after Edward Hall receives written notice of the premium from Anna Rogers for payment. Accompanying the first such written notification and any subsequent notifications informing of a change in the premium amount, Anna Rogers is ORDERED to provide Edward Hall with documentation from the carrier of the cost to Anna Rogers of providing coverage for the child.

If Policy Not Convertible - If the health insurance policy covering the child is not convertible and if no health insurance is available for the child through the employment or membership in a union, trade association, or other organization of either party, IT IS ORDERED that Edward Hall shall purchase and maintain, at his sole cost and expense, health insurance coverage for the child. _

Except as provided in paragraph 13 below, the party who is not carrying the health insurance policy covering the child is ORDERED to submit to the party carrying the policy, within ten days of receiving them, any and all forms, receipts, bills, and statements reflecting the health-care expenses the party not carrying the policy incurs on behalf of the child.

The party who is carrying the health insurance policy covering the child is ORDERED to submit all forms required by the insurance company for payment or reimbursement of health-care expenses incurred by either party on behalf of the child to the insurance carrier within ten days of that party's receiving any form, receipt, bill, or statement reflecting the expenses.

Constructive Trust for Payments Received - IT IS ORDERED that any insurance payments received by the party carrying the health insurance policy covering the child from the health insurance carrier as reimbursement for health-care expenses incurred by or on behalf of the child shall belong to the party who incurred and paid those expenses. IT IS FURTHER ORDERED that the party carrying the policy is designated a constructive trustee to receive any insurance checks or payments for health-care expenses incurred and paid by the other party, and the party carrying the policy shall endorse and forward the checks or payments, along with any explanation of benefits, to the other party within three days of receiving them.

Filing by Party Not Carrying Insurance - In accordance with article 3.51-13 of the Texas Insurance Code, IT IS ORDERED that the party who is not carrying the health insurance policy covering the child may, at that party's option, file directly with the insurance carrier with whom coverage is provided for the benefit of the child any claims for health-care expenses, including, but not limited to, medical, hospitalization, and dental costs.

Secondary Coverage - IT IS ORDERED that nothing in this decree shall prevent either party from providing secondary health insurance coverage for the child at that party's sole cost and expense. IT IS FURTHER ORDERED that if a party provides secondary health insurance coverage for the child, both parties shall cooperate fully with regard to the handling and filing of claims with the insurance carrier providing the coverage in order to maximize the benefits available to the child and to ensure that the party who pays for health-care expenses for the child is reimbursed for the payment from both carriers to the fullest extent possible.

Compliance with Insurance Company Requirements - Each party is ORDERED to conform to all requirements imposed by the terms and conditions of the policy of health insurance covering the child in order to assure maximum reimbursement or direct payment by the insurance company of the incurred health-care expense, including but not limited to requirements for advance notice to carrier, second opinions, and the like. Each party is ORDERED to attempt to use "preferred providers," or services within the health maintenance organization, if applicable; however, this provision shall not apply if emergency care is required. Disallowance of the bill by a health insurer shall not excuse the obligation of either party to make payment; however, if a bill is disallowed or the benefit reduced due to the failure of a party to follow procedures or requirements of the carrier, including the failure of a party to use a permitted provider in other than an emergency, that party shall be wholly responsible for the increased portion of that bill.

Except as provided above, each party is ORDERED to pay 50 percent of all reasonable and necessary health-care expenses not paid by insurance and incurred by or on behalf of the parties' child, including, without limitation, any copayments for office visits or prescription drugs, the yearly deductible, if any, and medical, surgical, prescription drug, mental health-care services, dental, eye care, ophthalmological, and orthodontic charges, for as long as child support is payable under the terms of this decree.

Exclusions - The provisions above concerning uninsured expenses shall not be interpreted to include expenses for travel to and from the health-care provider or nonprescription medication.

Reasonableness of Charges - IT IS ORDERED that reasonableness of the charges for health-care expenses shall be presumed on presentation of the bill to a party and that disallowance of the bill by a health insurer shall not excuse that party's obligation to make payment or reimbursement as otherwise provided herein.

. WARNING - A PARENT ORDERED TO PROVIDE HEALTH INSURANCE WHO FAILS TO DO SO IS LIABLE FOR NECESSARY MEDICAL EXPENSES OF THE CHILD, WITHOUT REGARD TO WHETHER THE EXPENSES WOULD HAVE BEEN PAID IF HEALTH INSURANCE HAD BEEN PROVIDED.

No Credit for Informal Payments.

IT IS ORDERED that the child support as prescribed in this order shall be exclusively discharged in the manner ordered and that any direct payments made by EDWARD HALL to ANNA ROGERS or any expenditures incurred by EDWARD HALL during EDWARD HALL's periods of possession of or access to the child, as prescribed in this order, for food, clothing, gifts, travel, shelter, or entertainment are deemed in addition to and not in lieu of the support ordered in this order.

Support as Obligation of Estate.

IT IS ORDERED that the provisions for child support in this order shall be an obligation of the estate of EDWARD HALL and shall not terminate on the death of EDWARD HALL. Payments received for the benefit of the child from the Social Security Administration, Department of Veterans Affairs, other government agency, or life insurance shall be a credit against this obligation.

Medical Notification.

Each party is ORDERED to inform the other party within twenty-four hours of any medical condition of the parties' child requiring surgical intervention, hospitalization, or both.

The Court finds that a proper showing has been made and that EDWARD HALL should be ordered to pay an equitable portion of all prenatal and postnatal health-care expenses of the mother and the child.

IT IS THEREFORE ORDERED that EDWARD HALL shall pay the prenatal and postnatal health-care expenses of the mother and the child as follows:

a.   Place: Urban Hospital

        Date: March 3, 1999

        Amount: $1500

IT IS ORDERED that the child formerly known as JUANA ROGERS shall hereafter be named JUANA ROGERS HALL.

The information required for each party by section 105.006(a) of the Texas Family Code is as follows:

Mother

Name: ANNA ROGERS

Social Security number: 111-11-1111

Driver's license number

      and issuing state: Texas Driver's License #123456

Current residence address: 111 Singleton St., Urban, Texas 77777

Mailing address: 111 Singleton St., Urban, Texas 77777

Home telephone number: 555-555-5567

Name of employer: Urban Fun Center

Address of employment: 1212 Main St., Urban, Texas 77777

Work telephone number: 555-555-6666

<u>Father</u>

Name: EDWARD HALL

Social Security number: 222-22-2222

Driver's license number and issuing state: Texas Driver's License #765432

Current residence address: 1212 Friendly, Urban, Texas 77777

Mailing address: 1212 Friendly, Urban, Texas 77777

Home telephone number: 555-555-4444

Name of employer: Urban Area Works

Address of employment: 3333 Hardy St., Urban, Texas 77777

Work telephone number: 555-555-0000

<u>Child</u>

Name: JUANA ROGERS

Social Security number: 333-33-3333

Driver's license number and issuing state: None

Current residence address: 111 Singleton St., Urban, Texas 77777

Mailing address: 111 Singleton St., Urban, Texas 77777

Home telephone number: 555-555-5567

Name of employer: None

Address of employment: N/A

Work telephone number: N/A

EACH PERSON WHO IS A PARTY TO THIS ORDER IS ORDERED TO NOTIFY EACH OTHER PARTY, THE COURT, AND THE STATE CASE REGISTRY OF ANY CHANGE IN THE PARTY'S CURRENT RESIDENCE ADDRESS, MAILING ADDRESS, HOME TELEPHONE NUMBER, NAME OF EMPLOYER, ADDRESS OF EMPLOY-MENT, DRIVER'S LICENSE NUMBER, AND WORK TELEPHONE NUMBER. THE PARTY IS ORDERED TO GIVE NOTICE OF AN INTENDED CHANGE IN ANY OF THE REQUIRED INFORMATION TO EACH OTHER PARTY, THE COURT, AND THE STATE CASE REGISTRY ON OR BEFORE THE 60TH DAY BEFORE THE INTENDED CHANGE. IF THE PARTY DOES NOT KNOW OR COULD NOT HAVE KNOWN OF THE CHANGE IN SUFFICIENT TIME TO PROVIDE 60-DAY NOTICE, THE PARTY IS ORDERED TO GIVE NOTICE OF THE CHANGE ON OR BEFORE THE FIFTH DAY AFTER THE DATE THAT THE PARTY KNOWS OF THE CHANGE.

THE DUTY TO FURNISH THIS INFORMATION TO EACH OTHER PARTY, THE COURT, AND THE STATE CASE REGISTRY CONTINUES AS LONG AS ANY PER-SON, BY VIRTUE OF THIS ORDER, IS UNDER AN OBLIGATION TO PAY CHILD

SUPPORT OR ENTITLED TO POSSESSION OF OR ACCESS TO A CHILD.

FAILURE BY A PARTY TO OBEY THE ORDER OF THIS COURT TO PROVIDE EACH OTHER PARTY, THE COURT, AND THE STATE CASE REGISTRY WITH THE CHANGE IN THE REQUIRED INFORMATION MAY RESULT IN FURTHER LITIGATION TO ENFORCE THE ORDER, INCLUDING CONTEMPT OF COURT. A FINDING OF CONTEMPT MAY BE PUNISHED BY CONFINEMENT IN JAIL FOR UP TO SIX MONTHS, A FINE OF UP TO $500 FOR EACH VIOLATION, AND A MONEY JUDGMENT FOR PAYMENT OF ATTORNEY'S FEES AND COURT COSTS.

Notice shall be given to the other party by delivering a copy of the notice to the party by registered or certified mail, return receipt requested. Notice shall be given to the Court by delivering a copy of the notice either in person to the clerk of this Court or by registered or certified mail addressed to the clerk. Notice shall be given to the state case registry by mailing a copy of the notice to State Case Registry, Central File Maintenance, P.O. Box 12048, Austin, Texas 78711-2048.

WARNINGS TO PARTIES: FAILURE TO OBEY A COURT ORDER FOR CHILD SUPPORT OR FOR POSSESSION OF OR ACCESS TO A CHILD MAY RESULT IN FURTHER LITIGATION TO ENFORCE THE ORDER, INCLUDING CONTEMPT OF COURT. A FINDING OF CONTEMPT MAY BE PUNISHED BY CONFINEMENT IN JAIL FOR UP TO SIX MONTHS, A FINE OF UP TO $500 FOR EACH VIOLATION, AND A MONEY JUDGMENT FOR PAYMENT OF ATTORNEY'S FEES AND COURT COSTS.

FAILURE OF A PARTY TO MAKE A CHILD SUPPORT PAYMENT TO THE PLACE AND IN THE MANNER REQUIRED BY A COURT ORDER MAY RESULT IN THE PARTY'S NOT RECEIVING CREDIT FOR MAKING THE PAYMENT.

FAILURE OF A PARTY TO PAY CHILD SUPPORT DOES NOT JUSTIFY DENYING THAT PARTY COURT-ORDERED POSSESSION OF OR ACCESS TO A CHILD. REFUSAL BY A PARTY TO ALLOW POSSESSION OF OR ACCESS TO A CHILD DOES NOT JUSTIFY FAILURE TO PAY COURT-ORDERED CHILD SUPPORT TO THAT PARTY.

IT IS ORDERED that all relief requested in this case and not expressly granted is denied.

SIGNED on _____.

_____
JUDGE PRESIDING

NO. 2212-99

IN THE INTEREST OF	§	IN THE DISTRICT COURT
	§	
JUANA ROGERS	§	001 JUDICIAL DISTRICT
	§	
A CHILD	§	URBAN COUNTY, TEXAS

NOTICE OF HEARING

Notice is hereby given that a hearing on the motion for parentage testing contained in the Petition to Establish Parentage will be held on _____, 2001, at ____ _.m. in the courtroom of the ___ District Court, _____ County Courthouse, ___ Texas.

Signed on: _____

_____
Judge or Clerk of the Court

STATEMENT ON ALTERNATIVE DISPUTE RESOLUTION

I AM AWARE THAT IT IS THE POLICY OF THE STATE OF TEXAS TO PROMOTE THE AMICABLE AND NONJUDICIAL SETTLEMENT OF DISPUTES INVOLVING CHILDREN AND FAMILIES. I AM AWARE OF ALTERNATIVE DISPUTE RESOLUTION METHODS INCLUDING MEDIATION. WHILE I RECOGNIZE THAT ALTERNATIVE DISPUTE RESOLUTION IS AN ALTERNATIVE TO AND NOT A SUBSTITUTE FOR A TRIAL AND THAT THIS CASE MAY BE TRIED IF IT IS NOT SETTLED, I REPRESENT TO THE COURT THAT I WILL ATTEMPT IN GOOD FAITH TO RESOLVE BEFORE FINAL TRIAL CONTESTED ISSUES IN THIS CASE BY ALTERNATIVE DISPUTE RESOLUTION WITHOUT THE NECESSITY OF COURT INTERVENTION.

_____

TYPICAL SUPPORT MODIFICATION CASE—CASE #3

The following hypothetical case is a story to apply to the forms that follow it. It is a fictitious scenario of a divorced couple to demonstrate how they could make changes in support and how the forms would be completed based on such a case. The forms that follow are how this couple would use them. Should you decide to fill them in for yourself, you will have to retype them with your information.

Mary and Donald Smith were previously divorced. Mary got custody and Donald was ordered to pay child support for their son, Anthony. After a few years, Mary learns that Donald has gotten a new job and is now making more money. She decides that it is time to take Donald back to court to have his child support raised. To begin the case, she files a PETITION TO MODIFY PARENT-CHILD RELATIONSHIP like that found in form 22. Mary must also attach a form 24, STATEMENT OF ALTERNATIVE DISPUTE RESOLUTION STATEMENT, with her own information to her petition. At the hearing, the judge sets Donald's child support based on the amount of money he is now making. Mary then prepares the ORDER IN SUIT TO MODIFY PARENT-CHILD RELATIONSHIP, using form 23. She will also need an employer's order to withhold income; the judge will sign that order at the same time as the modification order. (The order to withhold income is filled in like form 9 found on page 169, except Mary will use her own case style at the top in the interest of Anthony.)

TABLE OF FORMS FOR CASE #3

NO. 97-9999

IN THE INTEREST OF	§	IN THE DISTRICT COURT
	§	
ANTHONY SMITH	§	999TH JUDICIAL DISTRICT
	§	
A CHILD	§	WADE COUNTY, TEXAS

PETITION TO MODIFY PARENT-CHILD RELATIONSHIP

COMES NOW MARY SMITH, Petitioner, who is 45 years of age and resides at 82 Waterside Rd, Lakeview, Texas and files this Motion to Modify a prior order. Petitioner is the mother of the child and has standing to bring this suit. The requested modification will be in the best interest of the child.

The order to be modified is entitled Decree of Divorce and was rendered on October 31, 1997.

This Court has continuing, exclusive jurisdiction of this suit.

The following child is the subject of this suit:

Name: ANTHONY SMITH

Sex: Male

Birthplace: LAKEVIEW, TEXAS

Birth date: 12/25/1996

Present residence: with petitioner

The names and addresses of each party whose rights, privileges, duties, or powers may be affected by this motion are -

Name: DONALD SMITH

Age: 47

Address: 66 Wealthy Way, Lakeview, Texas 88888

Relationship: father

Process should be served at that address.

There has been no change of consequence in the status of the child's property since the prior order was rendered.

The circumstances of the child or a person affected by the order have materially and substantially changed since the rendition of the order to be modified, and the support payments previously ordered should be increased until the child is eighteen years of age and, if the child is fully enrolled in an accredited secondary school in a program leading toward a high school diploma or enrolled in courses for joint high school and junior college credit pursuant to Section 130.008 of the Texas Education Code, until the end of the month in which the child graduates from high school. Petitioner requests that any increase be made retroactive to the earlier of the time of service of citation on Respondent or the appearance of Respondent in this modification action.

Petitioner has signed a statement on alternative dispute resolution, which is attached as Exhibit 1.

Discovery will be conducted under level2.

Petitioner prays that citation and notice issue as required by law and that the Court enter its orders in accordance with the allegations contained in this petition.

Petitioner prays for general relief.

Mary Smith
82 Waterside
Lakeview, Texas 88888
555-555-6666
Petitioner

NO. 97-9999

IN THE INTEREST OF	§	IN THE DISTRICT COURT
	§	
ANTHONY SMITH	§	999TH JUDICIAL DISTRICT
	§	
A CHILD	§	WADE COUNTY, TEXAS

ORDER IN SUIT TO MODIFY PARENT-CHILD RELATIONSHIP

On _____ the Court heard this case.

Petitioner, MARY SMITH, appeared in person and announced ready for trial.

Respondent, DONALD SMITH, appeared in person and announced ready for trial.

The Court, after examining the record and the evidence and argument of counsel, finds that it has jurisdiction of this case and of all the parties and that no other court has continuing, exclusive jurisdiction of this case. All persons entitled to citation were properly cited.

A jury was waived, and all questions of fact and of law were submitted to the Court.

The Court finds that the following child is the subject of this suit:

Name: ANTHONY SMITH

Sex: Male

Birthplace: LAKEVIEW, TEXAS

Birth date: December 25, 1996

Present residence: with petitioner

Home state: Texas

The Court finds that the material allegations in the petition to modify are true and that the requested modification is in the best interest of the child. IT IS ORDERED that modification is GRANTED.

IT IS ORDERED that DONALD SMITH is obligated to pay and shall pay to MARY SMITH child support of $1200 per month, with the first payment being due and payable on September 1, 2001 and a like payment being due and payable on the first day of each month thereafter until the first month following the date of the earliest occurrence of one of the events specified below:

1.   the child reaches the age of eighteen years, provided that, if the child is fully enrolled in an accredited secondary school in a program leading toward a high school diploma or enrolled in courses for joint high school and junior college credit pursuant to Section

130.008 of the Texas Education Code, the periodic child-support payments shall continue to be due and paid until the end of the month in which the child graduates from high school;

2.   the child marries;

3.   the child dies;

4.   the child's disabilities are otherwise removed for general purposes;

5.   DONALD SMITH and MARY SMITH remarry each other; or

6.   further order modifying this child support.

Withholding from Earnings.

IT IS ORDERED that any employer of DONALD SMITH shall be ordered to withhold from earnings for child support from the disposable earnings of DONALD SMITH for the support of ANTHONY SMITH.

IT IS ORDERED that all payments shall be made through the Wade County Child Support Office, Wade County Courthouse, Lakeview, Texas 88888 and then remitted by that agency to MARY SMITH for the support of the child. IT IS FURTHER ORDERED that DONALD SMITH shall pay all fees charged by that agency.

IT IS FURTHER ORDERED that DONALD SMITH shall notify this Court and MARY SMITH by U.S. certified mail, return receipt requested, of any change of address and of any termination of employment. This notice shall be given no later than seven days after the change of address or the termination of employment. This notice or a subsequent notice shall also provide the current address of DONALD SMITH and the name and address of obligor's current employer, whenever that information becomes available.

IT IS ORDERED that, on the request of a prosecuting attorney, the attorney general, the friend of the Court, MARY SMITH, or DONALD SMITH, the clerk of this Court shall cause a certified copy of the "Order/Notice to Withhold Income for Child Support" to be delivered to any employer. IT IS FURTHER ORDERED that the clerk of this Court shall attach a copy of subchapter C of chapter 158 of the Texas Family Code for the information of any employer.

IT IS ORDERED that medical support shall be provided for the child as follows:

1.   the medical support provisions in the Decree of Divorce shall remain in full force and effect and are not being modified by this order.

No Credit for Informal Payments.

IT IS ORDERED that the child support as prescribed in this order shall be exclusively discharged in the manner ordered and that any direct payments made by DONALD SMITH to MARY SMITH or any expenditures incurred by DONALD SMITH during DONALD SMITH's periods of possession of or access to the child, as prescribed in this order, for food, clothing, gifts, travel, shelter, or entertainment are deemed in addition to and not in lieu of the support ordered in this order.

Support as Obligation of Estate.

IT IS ORDERED that the provisions for child support in this order shall be an obligation of the estate of DONALD SMITH and shall not terminate on the death of DONALD SMITH. Payments received for the benefit of the child from the Social Security Administration, Department of Veterans Affairs, other government agency, or life insurance shall be a credit against this obligation.

Medical Notification.

Each party is ORDERED to inform the other party within twenty-four hours of any medical condition of the parties' child requiring surgical intervention, hospitalization, or both.

Information Regarding Parties and Child.

The information required for each party by section 105.006(a) of the Texas Family Code is as follows:

Name: MARY SMITH
    Social Security number: 111-11-1111
    Driver's license number: 8237465
    Issuing state: Texas
    Current residence address: 82 Waterside Rd, Lakeview, Texas
    Mailing address: 82 Waterside Rd, Lakeview, Texas
    Home telephone number: 555/555-6666
    Name of employer: Wade Marine Supply
    Address of employment: 1212 Waterfront, Lakeview, Texas 88888
    Work telephone number: 555/555-2222

Name: DONALD SMITH
    Social Security number: 222-22-2222
    Driver's license number: 2873645
    Issuing state: Texas
    Current residence address: 66 Wealthy Way, Lakeview, Texas 88888
    Mailing address: 66 Wealthy Way, Lakeview, Texas 88888
    Home telephone number: 555-555-3333
    Name of employer: Superpower Computers

Address of employment: 22 Graphics St., Lakeview, Texas 88888
Work telephone number: 555-555-4444

Name: ANTHONY SMITH

Social Security number: 333-33-3333

Driver's license number: N/A

Issuing state: N/A

Current residence address: with petitioner

Mailing address: same as petitioner

Home telephone number: 555/555-6666

Name of employer: none

Address of employment: none

Work telephone number: none

EACH PERSON WHO IS A PARTY TO THIS ORDER IS ORDERED TO NOTIFY EACH OTHER PARTY, THE COURT, AND THE STATE CASE REGISTRY OF ANY CHANGE IN THE PARTY'S CURRENT RESIDENCE ADDRESS, MAILING ADDRESS, HOME TELEPHONE NUMBER, NAME OF EMPLOYER, ADDRESS OF EMPLOYMENT, DRIVER'S LICENSE NUMBER, AND WORK TELEPHONE NUMBER. THE PARTY IS ORDERED TO GIVE NOTICE OF AN INTENDED CHANGE IN ANY OF THE REQUIRED INFORMATION TO EACH OTHER PARTY, THE COURT, AND THE STATE CASE REGISTRY ON OR BEFORE THE 60TH DAY BEFORE THE INTENDED CHANGE. IF THE PARTY DOES NOT KNOW OR COULD NOT HAVE KNOWN OF THE CHANGE IN SUFFICIENT TIME TO PROVIDE 60-DAY NOTICE, THE PARTY IS ORDERED TO GIVE NOTICE OF THE CHANGE ON OR BEFORE THE FIFTH DAY AFTER THE DATE THAT THE PARTY KNOWS OF THE CHANGE.

THE DUTY TO FURNISH THIS INFORMATION TO EACH OTHER PARTY, THE COURT, AND THE STATE CASE REGISTRY CONTINUES AS LONG AS ANY PERSON, BY VIRTUE OF THIS ORDER, IS UNDER AN OBLIGATION TO PAY CHILD SUPPORT OR ENTITLED TO POSSESSION OF OR ACCESS TO A CHILD.

FAILURE BY A PARTY TO OBEY THE ORDER OF THIS COURT TO PROVIDE EACH OTHER PARTY, THE COURT, AND THE STATE CASE REGISTRY WITH THE CHANGE IN THE REQUIRED INFORMATION MAY RESULT IN FURTHER LITIGATION TO ENFORCE THE ORDER, INCLUDING CONTEMPT OF COURT. A FINDING OF CONTEMPT MAY BE PUNISHED BY CONFINEMENT IN JAIL FOR UP TO SIX MONTHS, A FINE OF UP TO $500 FOR EACH VIOLATION, AND A MONEY JUDGMENT FOR PAYMENT OF ATTORNEY'S FEES AND COURT COSTS.

Notice shall be given to the other party by delivering a copy of the notice to the party by registered or certified mail, return receipt requested. Notice shall be given to the Court by delivering a copy of the notice either in person to the clerk of this Court or by registered or certified mail addressed to the clerk. Notice shall be given to the state case registry by mailing a copy of the notice to State Case Registry, Central File Maintenance, P.O. Box 12048, Austin, Texas 78711-2048.

WARNINGS TO PARTIES: FAILURE TO OBEY A COURT ORDER FOR CHILD SUPPORT OR FOR POSSESSION OF OR ACCESS TO A CHILD MAY RESULT IN FURTHER LITIGATION TO ENFORCE THE ORDER, INCLUDING CONTEMPT OF COURT. A FINDING OF CONTEMPT MAY BE PUNISHED BY CONFINEMENT IN JAIL FOR UP TO SIX MONTHS, A FINE OF UP TO $500 FOR EACH VIOLATION, AND A MONEY JUDGMENT FOR PAYMENT OF ATTORNEY'S FEES AND COURT COSTS.

FAILURE OF A PARTY TO MAKE A CHILD SUPPORT PAYMENT TO THE PLACE AND IN THE MANNER REQUIRED BY A COURT ORDER MAY RESULT IN THE PARTY'S NOT RECEIVING CREDIT FOR MAKING THE PAYMENT.

FAILURE OF A PARTY TO PAY CHILD SUPPORT DOES NOT JUSTIFY DENYING THAT PARTY COURT-ORDERED POSSESSION OF OR ACCESS TO A CHILD. REFUSAL BY A PARTY TO ALLOW POSSESSION OF OR ACCESS TO A CHILD DOES NOT JUSTIFY FAILURE TO PAY COURT-ORDERED CHILD SUPPORT TO THAT PARTY.

IT IS ORDERED that the parties are discharged from the requirement of keeping and storing the documents produced in this case in accordance with rule 191.4(d) of the Texas Rules of Civil Procedure.

IT IS ORDERED that all relief requested in this case and not expressly granted is denied. All other terms of the prior orders not specifically modified in this order shall remain in full force and effect.

SIGNED on _____.

_____
JUDGE PRESIDING

APPROVED AND CONSENTED TO AS TO BOTH FORM AND SUBSTANCE:

_____
Petitioner

_____
Respondent

STATEMENT ON ALTERNATIVE DISPUTE RESOLUTION

I AM AWARE THAT IT IS THE POLICY OF THE STATE OF TEXAS TO PROMOTE THE AMICABLE AND NONJUDICIAL SETTLEMENT OF DISPUTES INVOLVING CHILDREN AND FAMILIES. I AM AWARE OF ALTERNATIVE DISPUTE RESOLUTION METHODS INCLUDING MEDIATION. WHILE I RECOGNIZE THAT ALTERNATIVE DISPUTE RESOLUTION IS AN ALTERNATIVE TO AND NOT A SUBSTITUTE FOR A TRIAL AND THAT THIS CASE MAY BE TRIED IF IT IS NOT SETTLED, I REPRESENT TO THE COURT THAT I WILL ATTEMPT IN GOOD FAITH TO RESOLVE BEFORE FINAL TRIAL CONTESTED ISSUES IN THIS CASE BY ALTERNATIVE DISPUTE RESOLUTION WITHOUT THE NECESSITY OF COURT INTERVENTION.

———————————————

TYPICAL VISITATION MODIFICATION CASE—CASE #4

The following hypothetical case is a story to apply to the forms that follow it. It is a ficti-tious scenario of a divorced couple to demonstrate how they could make changes in visita-tion and how the forms would be completed based on such a case. The forms that follow are how this couple would use them. Should you decide to fill them in for yourself, you will have to retype them with your information.

David and Donna Jones were married and had one son, Danny. They are now divorced, and David got primary possession of Danny. Donna has standard visitation. Donna has a new hus-band, Wally Tyler. David learns that Wally and Donna have been punishing Danny exces-sively, so David decides to take Donna back to court. He files a PETITION TO MODIFY PARENT-CHILD RELATIONSHIP like that in form 25, asking for Donna's visitation with Danny to be restricted. David must attach a form 25, STATEMENT ON ALTERNATIVE DISPUTE RESOLUTION with his own information to his petition. The judge enters an order requiring that Donna's visitation be supervised by her mother and also requiring Donna to be sure that Danny is never alone with Wally. David prepares a modification order, ORDER IN SUIT TO MODIFY PARENT-CHILD RELATIONSHIP using sample form 26 as his guide.

TABLE OF FORMS FOR CASE #4

NO. 8888-99

IN THE INTEREST OF	§	IN THE DISTRICT COURT
	§	
DANNY JONES	§	998TH JUDICIAL DISTRICT
	§	
A CHILD	§	PANHANDLE COUNTY, TEXAS

PETITION TO MODIFY PARENT-CHILD RELATIONSHIP

COMES NOW DAVID JONES, Petitioner, who is 40 years of age and resides at 122 Innocent Lane, Westtex, Texas and files this Motion to Modify. Petitioner is the father of the child and has standing to bring this suit. The requested modification will be in the best interest of the child.

The order to be modified is entitled Decree of Divorce and was rendered on December 31, 1999.

This Court has continuing, exclusive jurisdiction of this suit.

The following child is the subject of this suit:

Name: DANNY JONES

Sex: Male

Birthplace: Westtex, Texas

Birth date: 01/01/1998

Present residence: 1818 Mean Street, Westtex, Texas

The names and addresses of each party whose rights, privileges, duties, or powers may be affected by this motion are -

Name: DONNA JONES TYLER

Age: 39

Address: 100 Mean St., Westtex, Texas 22222

Relationship: mother

Process should be served at that address.

There has been no change of consequence in the status of the child's property since the prior order was rendered.

The circumstances of the child or a person affected by the order to be modified have materially and substantially changed since the rendition of the order. Petitioner requests that the terms and conditions for access to or possession of the child be modified to provide as follows: Respondent's visitation should be supervised. Petitioner would show the Court that

Respondent and her present husband, Wally Tyler, have been excessively punishing the child.

Petitioner requests the Court, after notice and hearing, to make temporary orders for the safety and welfare of the child, including but not limited to the following:

Denying Respondent access to the child or, alternatively, rendering a possession order in accordance with section 153.004(d)(2) of the Texas Family Code.

Petitioner requests the Court to dispense with the necessity of a bond, and Petitioner requests that, after notice and hearing, Respondent be further restrained and enjoined, pending the further order of the Court, from:

Removing the child beyond the jurisdiction of the Court, acting directly or in concert with others.

Disrupting or withdrawing the child from the school or day-care facility where the child is presently enrolled.

Hiding or secreting the child from Petitioner or changing the child's current place of abode at 100 Mean Street, Westtex, Texas.

Petitioner requests the Court, after trial on the merits, to grant the following permanent injunction:

a.   Respondent should be enjoined from having the child around her present husband, Wally Tyler.

Petitioner has signed a statement on alternative dispute resolution, which is attached as Exhibit 1.

Discovery will be conducted under level 2.

Petitioner prays that citation and notice issue as required by law and that the Court enter its orders in accordance with the allegations contained in this petition.

Petitioner prays that the Court, after notice and hearing, grant a temporary injunction enjoining Respondent, in conformity with the allegations of this petition, from the acts set forth above while this case is pending.

Petitioner prays that, on final hearing, the Court enter a permanent injunction enjoining Respondent, in conformity with the allegations of this petition, from the acts set forth above.

Petitioner prays for general relief.

David Jones
1212 Innocent
Westtex, Texas 22222
555-555-4321

NO. 8888-99

IN THE INTEREST OF	§	IN THE DISTRICT COURT
	§	
DANNY JONES	§	998TH JUDICIAL DISTRICT
	§	
A CHILD	§	PANHANDLE COUNTY, TEXAS

ORDER IN SUIT TO MODIFY PARENT-CHILD RELATIONSHIP

On _____ the Court heard this case.

Petitioner, DAVID JONES, appeared in person and announced ready for trial.

Respondent, DONNA JONES TYLER, appeared in person and announced ready for trial.

The Court, after examining the record and the evidence and argument of counsel, finds that it has jurisdiction of this case and of all the parties and that no other court has continuing, exclusive jurisdiction of this case. All persons entitled to citation were properly cited.

A jury was waived, and all questions of fact and of law were submitted to the Court.

The record of testimony was duly reported by the court reporter for the 998TH Judicial District Court.

The Court finds that the following child is the subject of this suit:

Name: DANNY JONES

Sex: Male

Birthplace: Westtex, Texas

Birth date: January 1, 1998

Present residence: 1818 Mean Street, Westtex, Texas

Home state: Texas

The Court finds that the material allegations in the petition to modify are true and that the requested modification is in the best interest of the child. IT IS ORDERED that modification is GRANTED.

IT IS ORDERED that Respondent's visitation shall be supervised by her mother, Sandy Lane, at all times.

<u>Permanent Injunctions as to Persons.</u>

The Court finds that, because of the conduct of DONNA JONES TYLER, a permanent injunction against her should be granted as appropriate relief because there is no adequate remedy at law.

The permanent injunction granted below shall be effective immediately and shall be binding on DONNA JONES TYLER; on her agents, servants, employees, and attorneys; and on those persons in active concert or participation with them who receive actual notice of this order by personal service or otherwise.

IT IS ORDERED that DONNA JONES TYLER is permanently enjoined from:

1.   allowing the child to be alone with Wally Tyler

Petitioner and Respondent waive issuance and service of the writ of injunction, by stipulation or as evidenced by the signatures below. IT IS ORDERED that Petitioner and Respondent shall be deemed to be duly served with the writ of injunction.

<u>Information Regarding Parties and Child.</u>

The information required for each party by section 105.006(a) of the Texas Family Code is as follows:

Name: DAVID JONES

> Social Security number: 111-11-1111
>
> Driver's license number: 123456578
>
> Issuing state: Texas
>
> Current residence address: 122 Innocent Lane, Westtex, Texas
>
> Mailing address: 122 Innocent Lane, Westtex, Texas
>
> Home telephone number: 555/555-5432
>
> Name of employer: Family Fun Store
>
> Address of employment: 1234 Main St., Westtex, Texas
>
> Work telephone number: 555-555-5678

Name: DONNA JONES TYLER

> Social Security number: 111-11-2222
>
> Driver's license number: 9753121
>
> Issuing state: Texas
>
> Current residence address: 100 Mean St., Westtex, Texas 22222

Mailing address: 100 Mean St., Westtex, Texas 22222

Home telephone number: 555-555-6777

Name of employer: Donnybrook

Address of employment: 5555 Side St., Westtex, Texas

Work telephone number: 555-555-9999

Name: DANNY JONES

Social Security number: 333-45-6789

Driver's license number: N/A

Issuing state: N/A

Current residence address: 100 Mean Street, Westtex, Texas

Mailing address: 1818 Mean Street, Westtex, Texas

Home telephone number: 555-555-9999

Name of employer: none

Address of employment: none

Work telephone number: none

EACH PERSON WHO IS A PARTY TO THIS ORDER IS ORDERED TO NOTIFY EACH OTHER PARTY, THE COURT, AND THE STATE CASE REGISTRY OF ANY CHANGE IN THE PARTY'S CURRENT RESIDENCE ADDRESS, MAILING ADDRESS, HOME TELEPHONE NUMBER, NAME OF EMPLOYER, ADDRESS OF EMPLOY-MENT, DRIVER'S LICENSE NUMBER, AND WORK TELEPHONE NUMBER. THE PARTY IS ORDERED TO GIVE NOTICE OF AN INTENDED CHANGE IN ANY OF THE REQUIRED INFORMATION TO EACH OTHER PARTY, THE COURT, AND THE STATE CASE REGISTRY ON OR BEFORE THE 60TH DAY BEFORE THE INTENDED CHANGE. IF THE PARTY DOES NOT KNOW OR COULD NOT HAVE KNOWN OF THE CHANGE IN SUFFICIENT TIME TO PROVIDE 60-DAY NOTICE, THE PARTY IS ORDERED TO GIVE NOTICE OF THE CHANGE ON OR BEFORE THE FIFTH DAY AFTER THE DATE THAT THE PARTY KNOWS OF THE CHANGE.

THE DUTY TO FURNISH THIS INFORMATION TO EACH OTHER PARTY, THE COURT, AND THE STATE CASE REGISTRY CONTINUES AS LONG AS ANY PER-SON, BY VIRTUE OF THIS ORDER, IS UNDER AN OBLIGATION TO PAY CHILD SUPPORT OR ENTITLED TO POSSESSION OF OR ACCESS TO A CHILD.

FAILURE BY A PARTY TO OBEY THE ORDER OF THIS COURT TO PROVIDE EACH OTHER PARTY, THE COURT, AND THE STATE CASE REGISTRY WITH THE CHANGE IN THE REQUIRED INFORMATION MAY RESULT IN FURTHER LITIGA-

TION TO ENFORCE THE ORDER, INCLUDING CONTEMPT OF COURT. A FINDING OF CONTEMPT MAY BE PUNISHED BY CONFINEMENT IN JAIL FOR UP TO SIX MONTHS, A FINE OF UP TO $500 FOR EACH VIOLATION, AND A MONEY JUDGMENT FOR PAYMENT OF ATTORNEY'S FEES AND COURT COSTS.

Notice shall be given to the other party by delivering a copy of the notice to the party by registered or certified mail, return receipt requested. Notice shall be given to the Court by delivering a copy of the notice either in person to the clerk of this Court or by registered or certified mail addressed to the clerk. Notice shall be given to the state case registry by mailing a copy of the notice to State Case Registry, Central File Maintenance, P.O. Box 12048, Austin, Texas 78711-2048.

WARNINGS TO PARTIES: FAILURE TO OBEY A COURT ORDER FOR CHILD SUPPORT OR FOR POSSESSION OF OR ACCESS TO A CHILD MAY RESULT IN FURTHER LITIGATION TO ENFORCE THE ORDER, INCLUDING CONTEMPT OF COURT. A FINDING OF CONTEMPT MAY BE PUNISHED BY CONFINEMENT IN JAIL FOR UP TO SIX MONTHS, A FINE OF UP TO $500 FOR EACH VIOLATION, AND A MONEY JUDGMENT FOR PAYMENT OF ATTORNEY'S FEES AND COURT COSTS.

FAILURE OF A PARTY TO MAKE A CHILD SUPPORT PAYMENT TO THE PLACE AND IN THE MANNER REQUIRED BY A COURT ORDER MAY RESULT IN THE PARTY'S NOT RECEIVING CREDIT FOR MAKING THE PAYMENT.

FAILURE OF A PARTY TO PAY CHILD SUPPORT DOES NOT JUSTIFY DENYING THAT PARTY COURT-ORDERED POSSESSION OF OR ACCESS TO A CHILD. REFUSAL BY A PARTY TO ALLOW POSSESSION OF OR ACCESS TO A CHILD DOES NOT JUSTIFY FAILURE TO PAY COURT-ORDERED CHILD SUPPORT TO THAT PARTY.

IT IS ORDERED that the parties are discharged from the requirement of keeping and storing the documents produced in this case in accordance with rule 191.4(d) of the Texas Rules of Civil Procedure.

IT IS ORDERED that all relief requested in this case and not expressly granted is denied. All other terms of the prior orders not specifically modified in this order shall remain in full force and effect.

SIGNED on _____.

_____
JUDGE PRESIDING

STATEMENT ON ALTERNATIVE DISPUTE RESOLUTION

I AM AWARE THAT IT IS THE POLICY OF THE STATE OF TEXAS TO PRO-MOTE THE AMICABLE AND NONJUDICIAL SETTLEMENT OF DISPUTES INVOLV-ING CHILDREN AND FAMILIES. I AM AWARE OF ALTERNATIVE DISPUTE RESO-LUTION METHODS INCLUDING MEDIATION. WHILE I RECOGNIZE THAT ALTERNATIVE DISPUTE RESOLUTION IS AN ALTERNATIVE TO AND NOT A SUB-STITUTE FOR A TRIAL AND THAT THIS CASE MAY BE TRIED IF IT IS NOT SET-TLED, I REPRESENT TO THE COURT THAT I WILL ATTEMPT IN GOOD FAITH TO RESOLVE BEFORE FINAL TRIAL CONTESTED ISSUES IN THIS CASE BY ALTER-NATIVE DISPUTE RESOLUTION WITHOUT THE NECESSITY OF COURT INTER-VENTION.

_____

INDEX

order, 8, 21, 24, 35, 39-40, 49, 50, 55, 63-68, 81, 105, 106, 110, 113-126

reporter, 73

rules, 4

testimony, 73

courtroom manners, 93-94

cross examination, 94

custody (conservatorship), 7, 17-28, 29-36, 38, 39, 40, 42, 43, 47, 51, 52, 77, 78, 79, 80, 81, 88, 98, 105, 111, 113, 114-120, 126

contested, 82, 118-120

joint, 17, 19, 27-28

joint managing, 51, 115-116, 120

modification, 114-120

possessory, 51

preference of the child, 18, 78

primary, 17, 47

sole, 27-28

sole managing, 114-115, 120

temporary, 30, 31-32

uncontested, 81

D

death, 20, 52, 60

default judgment. *See* judgment

Department of Protective and Regulatory Services, 20

depositions, 72-75

digest, 5

direct examination, 94

discipline, 19, 79

discovery, 71-77

divorce, 17, 18, 22, 23, 30, 35, 38, 52, 64, 66, 80, 81, 98, 101

grounds, 98

DNA testing, 38, 39-40

docket call system, 90

domestic violence. *See* abuse

due diligence, 27

E

emancipation, 19, 60

emergencies, 24, 80, 111-112, 118

employer's order to withhold from earnings for child support, 65, 169

enforcement, 105-110

evidence, 7, 28, 31, 71-80, 87-88, 89, 91, 92, 96, 117, 118, 121

expert witness. *See* witnesses

F

family bonds, 78

Family Court Services, 32

father, 21, 37, 38, 39, 41

biological, 37, 38, 41

legal, 41

presumed, 21

final decree of divorce, 28, 34, 97, 101, 148

final order in suit to establish parentage, 39, 97, 202

final orders, 8, 40-41, 49, 85, 95, 97, 101-102, 105, 118

finances, 79

financial information statement for hearings on temporary orders, 34, 55, 173

G

garnishment, 107

girlfriend. *See* overnight guests

grandparents, 20, 21, 48, 51-52

visitation, 51, 52

guardian ad litem, 63-64

guardians, 20, 24

H

hearing setting, 29, 30

hearsay, 87

I

illness, 79

income, 63

withholding, 63, 107

injunction, 30, 31, 50

insurance, 56, 66-67

health, 56, 66-67

medical, 66

Internet, 3, 5, 9, 27

interrogatories, 72, 75

J

judge, 18, 26, 27, 30, 33, 35, 39, 48, 55, 60, 65, 71, 72, 78, 80, 81, 88, 89, 90, 91, 92, 93, 94, 95, 97, 98, 101, 105, 106, 117

associate, 35

judgment, 35, 59, 96, 97-100, 106, 107-110

default, 35, 59, 97-100

jurisdiction, 20, 24, 25, 31, 50, 108, 114, 123

continuing, 24

emergency, 24

Your #1 Source for Real World Legal Information...

SPHINX® PUBLISHING
An Imprint of Sourcebooks, Inc.®

- Written by lawyers
- Simple English explanation of the law
- Forms and instructions included

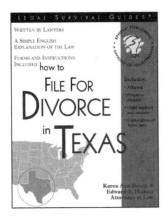

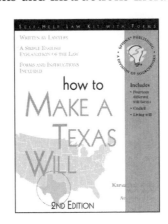

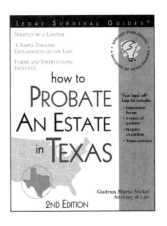

HOW TO FILE FOR DIVORCE IN TEXAS, 2ND ED.

Protect yourself by getting all the information you need about divorce laws and your legal rights in Texas. Whether you use a lawyer or not, you will find this book informative and helpful through a difficult process.

224 pages; $21.95;
ISBN 1-57071-330-8

HOW TO MAKE A TEXAS WILL, 2ND ED.

This book includes ready-to-use forms and instructions that take care of the many issues, such as Texas inheritance laws and joint property, that affect a will in Texas.

112 pages; $16.95;
ISBN 1-57071-417-7

HOW TO PROBATE AN ESTATE IN TEXAS, 2ND ED.

An easy-to-use handbook explaining the process of probate in Texas. Saves time, money, and frustration. Includes forms and instructions.

208 pages; $22.95;
ISBN 1-57071-418-5

See the following order form for books written specifically for California, Florida, Georgia, Illinois, Massachusetts, Michigan, Minnesota, New York, North Carolina, Ohio, Pennsylvania, and Texas!

What our customers say about our books:

"It couldn't be more clear for the lay person." —R.D.

"I want you to know I really appreciate your book. It has saved me a lot of time and money." —L.T.

"Your real estate contracts book has saved me nearly $12,000.00 in closing costs over the past year." —A.B.

"...many of the legal questions that I have had over the years were answered clearly and concisely through your plain English interpretation of the law." —C.E.H.

"If there weren't people out there like you I'd be lost. You have the best books of this type out there." —S.B.

"...your forms and directions are easy to follow." —C.V.M.

Sphinx Publishing's Legal Survival Guides
are directly available from Sourcebooks, Inc., or from your local bookstores.
For credit card orders call 1–800–432–7444, write P.O. Box 4410, Naperville, IL 60567-4410,
or fax 630-961-2168

SPHINX® PUBLISHING'S NATIONAL TITLES

Valid in All 50 States

LEGAL SURVIVAL IN BUSINESS

How to Form a Delaware Corporation from Any State	$24.95
How to Form a Limited Liability Company	$22.95
Incorporate in Nevada from Any State	$24.95
How to Form a Nonprofit Corporation	$24.95
How to Form Your Own Corporation (3E)	$24.95
How to Form Your Own Partnership	$22.95
How to Register Your Own Copyright (3E)	$21.95
How to Register Your Own Trademark (3E)	$21.95
Most Valuable Business Legal Forms You'll Ever Need (3E)	$21.95
Most Valuable Corporate Forms You'll Ever Need (2E)	$24.95

LEGAL SURVIVAL IN COURT

Crime Victim's Guide to Justice (2E)	$21.95
Grandparents' Rights (3E)	$24.95
Help Your Lawyer Win Your Case (2E)	$14.95
Jurors' Rights (2E)	$12.95
Legal Research Made Easy (2E)	$16.95
Winning Your Personal Injury Claim (2E)	$24.95
Your Rights When You Owe Too Much	$16.95

LEGAL SURVIVAL IN REAL ESTATE

Essential Guide to Real Estate Contracts	$18.95
Essential Guide to Real Estate Leases	$18.95
How to Buy a Condominium or Townhome	$19.95

LEGAL SURVIVAL IN PERSONAL AFFAIRS

Cómo Hacer su Propio Testamento	$16.95
Guía de Inmigración a Estados Unidos (2E)	$24.95
Cómo Solicitar su Propio Divorcio	$24.95
How to File Your Own Bankruptcy (4E)	$21.95
How to File Your Own Divorce (4E)	$24.95
How to Make Your Own Will (2E)	$16.95
How to Write Your Own Living Will (2E)	$16.95
How to Write Your Own Premarital Agreement (2E)	$21.95
How to Win Your Unemployment Compensation Claim	$21.95
Living Trusts and Simple Ways to Avoid Probate (2E)	$22.95
Most Valuable Personal Legal Forms You'll Ever Need	$24.95
Neighbor v. Neighbor (2E)	$16.95
The Nanny and Domestic Help Legal Kit	$22.95
The Power of Attorney Handbook (3E)	$19.95
Repair Your Own Credit and Deal with Debt	$18.95
The Social Security Benefits Handbook (3E)	$18.95
Unmarried Parents' Rights	$19.95
U.S.A. Immigration Guide (3E)	$19.95
Your Right to Child Custody, Visitation and Support (2E)	$24.95

Legal Survival Guides are directly available from Sourcebooks, Inc., or from your local bookstores.
Prices are subject to change without notice.

For credit card orders call 1–800–432–7444, write P.O. Box 4410, Naperville, IL 60567-4410
or fax 630-961-2168

SPHINX® PUBLISHING ORDER FORM

BILL TO:		SHIP TO:	
Phone #	Terms	F.O.B. Chicago, IL	Ship Date

Charge my: ☐ VISA ☐ MasterCard ☐ American Express

☐ **Money Order or Personal Check**

Credit Card Number

Expiration Date

Qty	ISBN	Title	Retail	Ext.
		SPHINX PUBLISHING NATIONAL TITLES		
___	1-57248-148-X	Cómo Hacer su Propio Testamento	$16.95	___
___	1-57248-147-1	Cómo Solicitar su Propio Divorcio	$24.95	___
___	1-57248-163-3	Crime Victim's Guide to Justice (2E)	$21.95	___
___	1-57248-159-5	Essential Guide to Real Estate Contracts	$18.95	___
___	1-57248-160-9	Essential Guide to Real Estate Leases	$18.95	___
___	1-57248-139-0	Grandparents' Rights (3E)	$24.95	___
___	1-57248-087-4	Guía de Inmigración a Estados Unidos (2E)	$24.95	___
___	1-57248-103-X	Help Your Lawyer Win Your Case (2E)	$14.95	___
___	1-57071-164-X	How to Buy a Condominium or Townhome	$19.95	___
___	1-57071-223-9	How to File Your Own Bankruptcy (4E)	$21.95	___
___	1-57248-132-3	How to File Your Own Divorce (4E)	$24.95	___
___	1-57248-100-5	How to Form a DE Corporation from Any State	$24.95	___
___	1-57248-083-1	How to Form a Limited Liability Company	$22.95	___
___	1-57248-099-8	How to Form a Nonprofit Corporation	$24.95	___
___	1-57248-133-1	How to Form Your Own Corporation (3E)	$24.95	___
___	1-57071-343-X	How to Form Your Own Partnership	$22.95	___
___	1-57248-119-6	How to Make Your Own Will (2E)	$16.95	___
___	1-57248-124-2	How to Register Your Own Copyright (3E)	$21.95	___
___	1-57248-104-8	How to Register Your Own Trademark (3E)	$21.95	___
___	1-57071-349-9	How to Win Your Unemployment Compensation Claim	$21.95	___
___	1-57248-118-8	How to Write Your Own Living Will (2E)	$16.95	___
___	1-57071-344-8	How to Write Your Own Premarital Agreement (2E)	$21.95	___
___	1-57248-158-7	Incorporate in Nevada from Any State	$24.95	___
___	1-57071-333-2	Jurors' Rights (2E)	$12.95	___
___	1-57071-400-2	Legal Research Made Easy (2E)	$16.95	___
___	1-57071-336-7	Living Trusts and Simple Ways to Avoid Probate (2E)	$22.95	___
___	1-57248-167-6	Most Valuable Bus. Legal Forms You'll Ever Need (3E)	$21.95	___
___	1-57071-346-4	Most Valuable Corporate Forms You'll Ever Need (2E)	$24.95	___
___	1-57248-130-7	Most Valuable Personal Legal Forms You'll Ever Need	$24.95	___
___	1-57248-098-X	The Nanny and Domestic Help Legal Kit	$22.95	___
___	1-57248-089-0	Neighbor v. Neighbor (2E)	$16.95	___
___	1-57071-348-0	The Power of Attorney Handbook (3E)	$19.95	___
___	1-57248-149-8	Repair Your Own Credit and Deal with Debt	$18.95	___
___	1-57248-168-4	The Social Security Benefits Handbook (3E)	$18.95	___
___	1-57071-399-5	Unmarried Parents' Rights	$19.95	___
___	1-57071-354-5	U.S.A. Immigration Guide (3E)	$19.95	___
___	1-57248-138-2	Winning Your Personal Injury Claim (2E)	$24.95	___
___	1-57248-162-5	Your Right to Child Custody, Visitation and Support (2E)	$24.95	___
___	1-57248-157-9	Your Rights When You Owe Too Much	$16.95	___
		CALIFORNIA TITLES		
___	1-57248-150-1	CA Power of Attorney Handbook (2E)	$18.95	___
___	1-57248-151-X	How to File for Divorce in CA (3E)	$26.95	___
___	1-57071-356-1	How to Make a CA Will	$16.95	___
___	1-57248-145-5	How to Probate and Settle an Estate in California	$26.95	___
___	1-57248-146-3	How to Start a Business in CA	$18.95	___
___	1-57071-358-8	How to Win in Small Claims Court in CA	$16.95	___
___	1-57071-359-6	Landlords' Rights and Duties in CA	$21.95	___
		FLORIDA TITLES		
___	1-57071-363-4	Florida Power of Attorney Handbook (2E)	$16.95	___
___	1-57248-093-9	How to File for Divorce in FL (6E)	$24.95	___
___	1-57071-380-4	How to Form a Corporation in FL (4E)	$24.95	___
___	1-57248-086-6	How to Form a Limited Liability Co. in FL	$22.95	___
___	1-57071-401-0	How to Form a Partnership in FL	$22.95	___
___	1-57248-113-7	How to Make a FL Will (6E)	$16.95	___

Form Continued on Following Page   **SUBTOTAL**

To order, call Sourcebooks at 1-800-432-7444 or FAX (630) 961-2168 (Bookstores, libraries, wholesalers—please call for discount)

Prices are subject to change without notice.

SPHINX® PUBLISHING ORDER FORM

Qty	ISBN	Title	Retail	Ext.
	1-57248-088-2	How to Modify Your FL Divorce Judgment (4E)	$24.95	
	1-57248-144-7	How to Probate and Settle an Estate in FL (4E)	$26.95	
	1-57248-081-5	How to Start a Business in FL (5E)	$16.95	
	1-57071-362-6	How to Win in Small Claims Court in FL (6E)	$16.95	
	1-57248-123-4	Landlords' Rights and Duties in FL (8E)	$21.95	

GEORGIA TITLES

Qty	ISBN	Title	Retail	Ext.
	1-57248-137-4	How to File for Divorce in GA (4E)	$21.95	
	1-57248-075-0	How to Make a GA Will (3E)	$16.95	
	1-57248-140-4	How to Start a Business in Georgia (2E)	$16.95	

ILLINOIS TITLES

Qty	ISBN	Title	Retail	Ext.
	1-57071-405-3	How to File for Divorce in IL (2E)	$21.95	
	1-57071-415-0	How to Make an IL Will (2E)	$16.95	
	1-57071-416-9	How to Start a Business in IL (2E)	$18.95	
	1-57248-078-5	Landlords' Rights & Duties in IL	$21.95	

MASSACHUSETTS TITLES

Qty	ISBN	Title	Retail	Ext.
	1-57248-128-5	How to File for Divorce in MA (3E)	$24.95	
	1-57248-115-3	How to Form a Corporation in MA	$24.95	
	1-57248-108-0	How to Make a MA Will (2E)	$16.95	
	1-57248-106-4	How to Start a Business in MA (2E)	$18.95	
	1-57248-107-2	Landlords' Rights and Duties in MA (2E)	$21.95	

MICHIGAN TITLES

Qty	ISBN	Title	Retail	Ext.
	1-57071-409-6	How to File for Divorce in MI (2E)	$21.95	
	1-57248-077-7	How to Make a MI Will (2E)	$16.95	
	1-57071-407-X	How to Start a Business in MI (2E)	$16.95	

MINNESOTA TITLES

Qty	ISBN	Title	Retail	Ext.
	1-57248-142-0	How to File for Divorce in MN	$21.95	

NEW YORK TITLES

Qty	ISBN	Title	Retail	Ext.
	1-57248-141-2	How to File for Divorce in NY (2E)	$26.95	
	1-57248-105-6	How to Form a Corporation in NY	$24.95	
	1-57248-095-5	How to Make a NY Will (2E)	$16.95	
	1-57071-185-2	How to Start a Business in NY	$18.95	
	1-57071-187-9	How to Win in Small Claims Court in NY	$16.95	
	1-57071-186-0	Landlords' Rights and Duties in NY	$21.95	

Qty	ISBN	Title	Retail	Ext.
	1-57071-188-7	New York Power of Attorney Handbook	$19.95	
	1-57248-122-6	Tenants' Rights in NY	$21.95	

NORTH CAROLINA TITLES

Qty	ISBN	Title	Retail	Ext.
	1-57071-326-X	How to File for Divorce in NC (2E)	$22.95	
	1-57248-129-3	How to Make a NC Will (3E)	$16.95	
	1-57248-184-6	How to Start a Business in NC (3E)	$18.95	
	1-57248-091-2	Landlords' Rights & Duties in NC	$21.95	

OHIO TITLES

Qty	ISBN	Title	Retail	Ext.
	1-57248-190-0	How to File for Divorce in OH (2E)	$24.95	
	1-57248-174-9	How to Form a Corporation in Ohio	$24.95	

PENNSYLVANIA TITLES

Qty	ISBN	Title	Retail	Ext.
	1-57248-127-7	How to File for Divorce in PA (2E)	$24.95	
	1-57248-094-7	How to Make a PA Will (2E)	$16.95	
	1-57248-112-9	How to Start a Business in PA (2E)	$18.95	
	1-57071-179-8	Landlords' Rights and Duties in PA	$19.95	

TEXAS TITLES

Qty	ISBN	Title	Retail	Ext.
	1-57248-171-4	Child Custody, Visitation, and Support in TX	$22.95	
	1-57071-330-8	How to File for Divorce in TX (2E)	$21.95	
	1-57248-114-5	How to Form a Corporation in TX (2E)	$24.95	
	1-57071-417-7	How to Make a TX Will (2E)	$16.95	
	1-57071-418-5	How to Probate an Estate in TX (2E)	$22.95	
	1-57071-365-0	How to Start a Business in TX (2E)	$18.95	
	1-57248-111-0	How to Win in Small Claims Court in TX (2E)	$16.95	
	1-57248-110-2	Landlords' Rights and Duties in TX (2E)	$21.95	

SUBTOTAL THIS PAGE _____

SUBTOTAL PREVIOUS PAGE _____

Shipping — $5.00 for 1st book, $1.00 each additional _____

Illinois residents add 6.75% sales tax _____

Connecticut residents add 6.00% sales tax _____

TOTAL _____

To order, call Sourcebooks at 1-800-432-7444 or FAX (630) 961-2168 (Bookstores, libraries, wholesalers—please call for discount)

Prices are subject to change without notice.